Conclusion of Junior English, Series of Get Ready Jump

KB249649

★ **Basic Dialogue**

★ **Listening Practice Pages**

★ **Writing Practice Pages**

★ **Homework**

★ **Evaluation Exam**

Jump

Get Ready

1

Author • Samuel Lee | Hyunjee Shim • Editorial Supervisor • LLS English Research Center

J PLUS
Language Publishing Co.

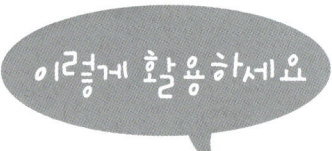

Tips

1) Time allotment 1회 50분 수업의 알찬 진행을 위해 매 페이지마다 수업 진행시간이 표기되어 있습니다.
2) Writing Practice Pages(Express Yourself): 매 과의 중심 단어와 표현을 써 볼 수 있는 페이지입니다.
3) Evaluation Exam: 각 8과씩 공부한 후 중간 학습 평가 시험을, 최종 Final Test를 통해 학생들의 실력을 평가할 수 있습니다.
4) Audio Script: 웹사이트에서 모든 과의 대화와 리스닝 문제를 다운 받아 사용하실 수 있습니다.

각 과의 구성

1) Dialogue: 중요 표현과 단어들을 제시했습니다. 롤플레이로 본문 속 주인공들이 되어 재미있게 말해 보세요.
2) Let's Practice: 문제를 듣고 풀며 배운 내용을 확인해 보세요.
3) Sight Word Zone: 그 과에서 꼭 알아두어야 할 단어입니다. 정확한 발음과 철자를 익혀 유창한 English Reading의 기초를 다져 보세요.
4) Check & Check: Sight Word에서 배운 단어들을 다양한 형태의 문제들로 한번 더 꼼꼼히 확인해 보세요.
5) Let's Play: 재미있는 액티비티로 배운 내용을 다양한 방법으로 말해 보세요.
6) Let's Do It At Home: 숙제를 하거나 수업시간에 복습용으로 활용하세요.

Get Ready Jump

Samuel Lee

Hello and welcome to the Get Ready Jump series of books!

This thoughtful series will give children a fun and interactive means of learning English.

The wonderful illustrations will engage youngsters whilst exposing them to foreign cultures and teach them about grammar usage.

Of course there is the requisite balanced exploration of the 4 main arenas in studying English: speaking, listening, writing and reading.

But the Get Ready Jump series of books endeavors to enrich the lives of children by making learning a joyful experience.

Hyunjee Shim

"Get Ready Jump 1"은 "Get Ready" 다음 단계로서, 영어 학습의 업그레이드를 경험할 수 있습니다. 어린이들이 일상 생활에서 접할 수 있는 상황을 등장인물들이 재미있게 엮어나가며 어린이들이 생활에서 표현하고 싶었던 내용들을 다양하게 제시하고 역할극, 노래, 챈트, 게임 등을 통해 다양한 표현들을 자연스럽게 습득하도록 하였습니다.

본 "Get Ready Jump 1"은 듣기와 말하기를 중심으로 읽기, 쓰기까지 다양한 활동으로 언어의 네 가지 영역을 균형 있게 학습하도록 짜여진 교재입니다.

특히 대화 내용과 주요 표현들을 반복적으로 오디오를 통해 학습할 수 있도록 하였고, Homework로 집에서 학습 내용을 복습할 수 있는 한편, 진도에 따라 Test를 통해 학습 성과를 점검할 수 있도록 하였습니다.

언어는 일상생활 속에서 자신의 의사를 표현하는 도구입니다. "Get Ready Jump 1"로 영어를 접하는 어린이들이 자신감을 가지고 자신의 뜻을 바르게 전달하며 풍성한 표현과 생각을 통해 더 큰 미래를 펼칠 수 있기를 바랍니다.

Get Ready Jump

Contents

My Brother Mike Is Tall And Fat

DATE /

What's this?

This is a picture of my family.

①

Alice: Can I see it? Who's this boy?

Scott: That is my brother. His name is Mike.

Alice: He looks tall and fat. Who's this girl?

Scott: That is my sister. Her name is Carol.

Alice: She looks so pretty.

I have a brother and his name is Mike.

He looks tall and fat.

brother / Mike
tall / fat

sister / Carol
short / pretty

father / Henry
smart

mother / Nancy
wise / kind

2

Scott: Do you have any sisters?

Alice: Yes, I do. I have a sister Louise. I can show you her picture.

Scott: Is this your sister? She looks short and pretty.

She looks just like you!
This is you!

No! We're twins!

baby sister / Amy
young / cute

grandfather / Jack
old / thin

grandmother / Helen
old / healthy

uncle / Andy
strong / funny

Let's Practice

 Listen and choose the correct person.

A	B	A	B	A	B

Sight Word Zone!

 Listen and repeat.

a	an	he
she	boy	girl

Let's trace and write.

a a a a

an an an an

he he he he

she she she she

boy boy boy boy

girl girl girl girl

Check & Check

15 min

4 Listen and fill in the blanks.

1. I have ☐ brother. ☐ is ☐ good student.

2. I have ☐ aunt. ☐ wants ☐ ice cream cone.

3. My brother has ☐ chicken, ☐ alligator and ☐ elephant.

4. My aunt has ☐ pencil, ☐ eraser and ☐ ruler.

WORD BOX   a   an   a   She   an   a   a   a   He   an   an   an

Check the missing words and write them.

a
an
he
she
girl
boy

he girl
boy she
a

an
_____

girl he
boy a
_____

boy he
a
_____

he
_____

a he
_____

Let's **Play** 10 min

You Need — a die — markers

Sentence Race

Repair

brother

tall

fat

father

+1

grandfather Repair

thin

strong

short

-1

old

mother

grandmother

kind

smart

aunt

FINISH!

hairy

START here!

+2

young

Exchange

pretty

sister

ugly

〈Tips!〉 주사위를 굴려서 숫자만큼 말을 이동하여 칸에 해당하는 단어를 사용하여 가족 구성원에 대해 표현하는 게임입니다. "Repair"에서는 한 번 쉬고 "Exchange"에서는 상대방의 말과 자리를 바꿀 수 있습니다.

Let's Do It At Home

1. Listen and circle.

A   B

A   B

2. Unscramble the sentences.

1

My / . / looks / grandfather / and / old / thin

_____.

2

sister / . / tall / My / looks / pretty / and

_____.

3

and / looks / My / fat / . / father / tall

_____.

3. Choose the right words and fill in the blanks.

I have _____ a/an _____ uncle/aunt.

Her name is Julie.

_____ She/ He is _____ a/an violinist.

_____ He/She looks so pretty.

_____ He/She wants _____ a/an ice cream

cone like me. We like ice cream!

Mom Is Cooking In The Kitchen

6

❷

Scott: The baby must be hungry. Where's mom?

Amy: Maybe she's in the garden.

Scott: What's she doing there?

Amy: She's watering the plants.

❶

Scott: Mom! Mom! The baby is crying!

Amy: What happened?

❸

Scott: Mom is not in the garden.

Role play

❶ Where is your dad?

❷ He's in the garden.

❸ What's he doing?

❹ He's watering the plants.

sister

in the bathroom
taking a shower

brother

in the bedroom
sleeping

④

Scott: Mom is not in the bathroom.

⑤

Scott: Mom! You're in my bedroom!
What are you doing here?

Mom: I'm cleaning your bedroom.

⑥ Scott: Phew! She fell asleep. Mom, now I feel so hungry.

grandfather	uncle	grandmother	mother

in the living room reading a newspaper	in the yard fixing a car	in the kitchen cooking dinner	in the dining room feeding the baby

Let's Practice

7 Listen and number in order.

Sight Word Zone!

 **8** Listen and repeat.

as	by	has
at	goes	is

Let's trace and write.

as as as as

by by by by

has has has has

at at at at

goes goes goes goes

is is is is

Check & Check

15 min

9 **Listen and fill in the blanks.**

1. My sister Sue [____] to school [____] bicycle.

2. She [____] to the zoo [____] bus.

3. My brother Joey [____] a student [____] this school.

4. He [____] lunch [____] noon.

5. My best friend Dan [____] [____] many books [____] I have.

6. He [____] [____] tall [____] I am.

WORD BOX   by   at   is   as   has   by   as   at   goes   is   as   as   goes   has

Follow the lines to connect each letter cluster. Then write.

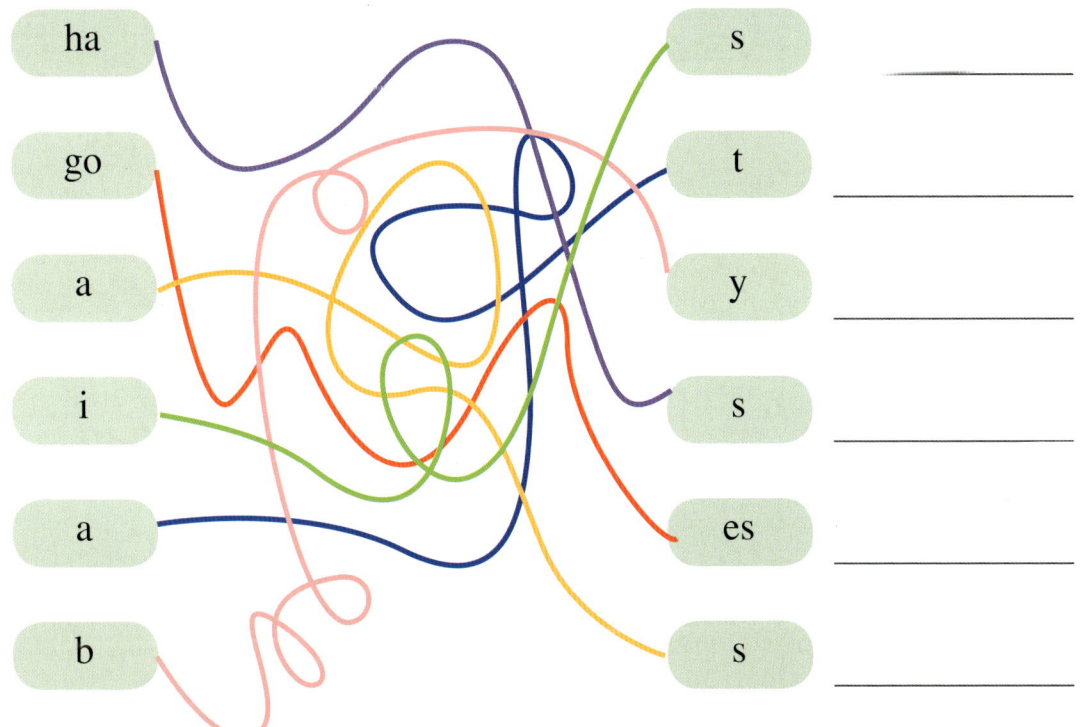

ha		s	_____
go		t	_____
a		y	_____
i		s	_____
a		es	_____
b		s	_____

Let's **Play**

10 min

You Need scissors

Where are they?

cooking	watering the plants	eating dinner
watching TV	sleeping	taking a shower
kitchen	garden	dining room
living room	bedroom	bathroom

ex

cooking + kitchen

↳ My mother is cooking in the kitchen.

〈Tips!〉 두 명씩 한 팀이 되어 카드를 잘라 모두 뒤집어 놓고, 두 개씩 골라 뒤집을 때 행동과 장소가 나오면
"_____ is _____ in the _____"라고 말하면 카드를 가지고 갈 수 있습니다. 단 같은 종류인 경우는 가지고 갈 수 없습니다.
(예: cooking과 eating dinner, 또는 bathroom과 garden)

Let's Do It At Home

 1. Listen and correctly place in the word stickers. Sticker

① 　② 　③

④ 　⑤ 　⑥

2. Read and match.

❶ My uncle is sleeping in his bedroom.

❷ My mom is cooking in the kitchen.

❸ My grandpa is watching TV in the living room.

ⓐ

ⓑ

ⓒ

3. Unscramble the sentences.

❶ is / ? / mom / What / doing / your

_____

❷ She / . / cleaning / the / in / is / bedroom

_____

I Want A Red Skirt

DATE /

❶

Clerk: Hi, there. May I help you?

Tina: Yes, I'm looking for a skirt.

❷

Clerk: What color do you want?

Tina: I don't know. Could you show me some different skirts?

Role play

❷ I want a blouse.

❶ What are you looking for?

❸ What color do you want?

❹ I want a green polka dot blouse.

a navy baseball cap

a yellow green necktie

a brown stripe skirt

❸

Clerk: Let's try a yellow skirt? It's new.

Tina: My shirt has blue stripes. It's not good with this skirt.

❹

Clerk: How about black? You'll look slim.

Tina: No thanks. Black is too dark.

Clerk: Then, what color do you want?

Tina: I will try red.

❺

Clerk: It's great on you!

Tina: Thanks! I really want this red skirt!

❷ I want sandals.

❶ May I help you?

❸ What color do you want?

❹ I will try the pink sandals.

yellow and gray sneakers

sky blue jeans

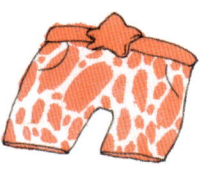

red dotted shorts

❋Let's Practice

 Listen and choose the correct clothes.

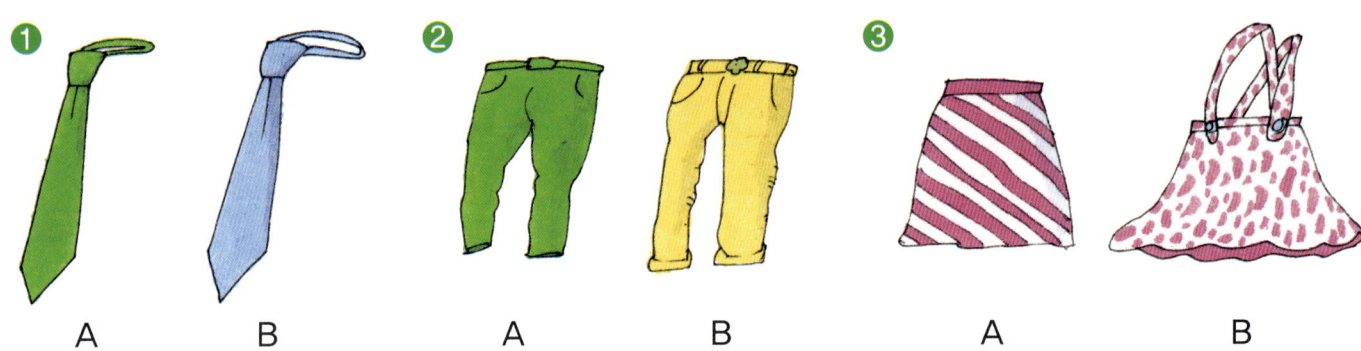

❶ A B ❷ A B ❸ A B

ⓢight Word Zone!

 Listen and repeat.

it	was	the
to	little	have

Let's trace and write.

it it it it

was was was was

the the the the

to to to to

little little little little

have have have have

Check & Check 15 min

 Listen and fill in the blanks by choosing the proper words.

1. The boy _____ is / was _____ at / to school yesterday.

2. I _____ is / was riding a bicycle yesterday.

   But today I'm at home. I _____ have / had a cold.

3. The girl _____ is / was playing _____ a / the violin.

   She sounds like _____ a / the great violinist.

4. I _____ have / has some flowers in my garden.

   My garden _____ is / was full of _____ little / big flowers.

Circle the words in each letter soup and write.

bfrupehavesy

rtojekolsiptew

gerjmuwdwas

qtlittleomscvu

fgdrtmrjgthek

bprefityinveo

Cut and Play

Make your own doll.

You Need | scissors | glue | colored pencils

 **Useful** Expressions

a red ribbon

a brown bag

a blue bag

a blue cap

a pink cap

a sky blue cape

a purple skirt

a green training jacket

training pants

jean pants

〈Tips!〉 그림의 인형들에게 색칠을 하고 인형이 어떤 옷을 입었는지 각자 말해 보는 시간을 가진 후, 인형을 가지고 Role Play를 합니다.

Let's Do It At Home

1. Read and write the names.

① I'm Tina. I'm looking for a baseball cap. I want it in red.

② I'm Scott. I want a necktie for my dad. I want a blue striped one.

③ I'm Bob. I want sneakers. I will try them in purple and grey.

④ I'm Alice. I'm looking for sandals. I will try yellow green sandals.

2. Listen and write the words.

 15

① Joey _____ sick yesterday.
He _____ healthy today.

② I _____ a brother.
My cousin _____ a sister.

3. Write the words in the puzzle.

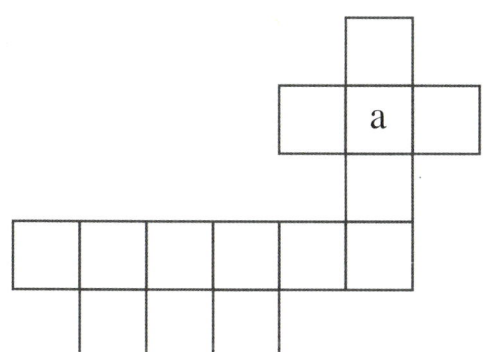

a

it
was
to
little
have

Unit 4

I Get Up At 7:40 In The Morning

DATE /

①

Max: What time do you get up?

Alice: I get up at 7:40 in the morning.

②

Max: What time do you wash your face?

Alice: I wash my face at 8:10 in the morning.

③

Max: What time do you have breakfast?

Alice: I have breakfast at 8:20 in the morning.

Role play

What time do you make your bed?

make bed/ 7:50 in the morning

I make my bed at 7:50 in the morning.

brush teeth / 8:00 in the morning

have lunch / 12:10 in the afternoon

4

Max: What time do you get dressed?

Alice: I get dressed at 8:30 in the morning.

5

Max: What time do you go to school?

Alice: I go to school at 8:50 in the morning.

6

"MAX! NO!"

Alice: Oh, my! It's 9:10. I'm late!

do homework / 3:20
in the afternoon

have dinner / 6:30
in the evening

go to bed / 9:40
at night

⭐ Let's Practice

 17 Listen. If the picture is correct, write **O**. But if not, then write **X**.

🌀 Sight Word Zone!

 18 Listen and repeat.

I	am	run
fast	down	has

Let's trace and write.

I I I I

am am am am

run run run run

fast fast fast fast

down down down down

has has has has

Check & Check

15 min

19 Listen and fill in the blanks by choosing the proper words.

①  I _____ have / has breakfast at 8:10.
My grandma _____ have / has breakfast with me.

②  I _____ am / have late!
I _____ walk / run to school.

③  Max goes _____ up / down .
Alice goes _____ up / down .

Alice

Max

Trace each letter and make words with them.

a
m

u
n r

a
s
t
f

d
o
w n

s
h a

h a
v
e

Spin and say.

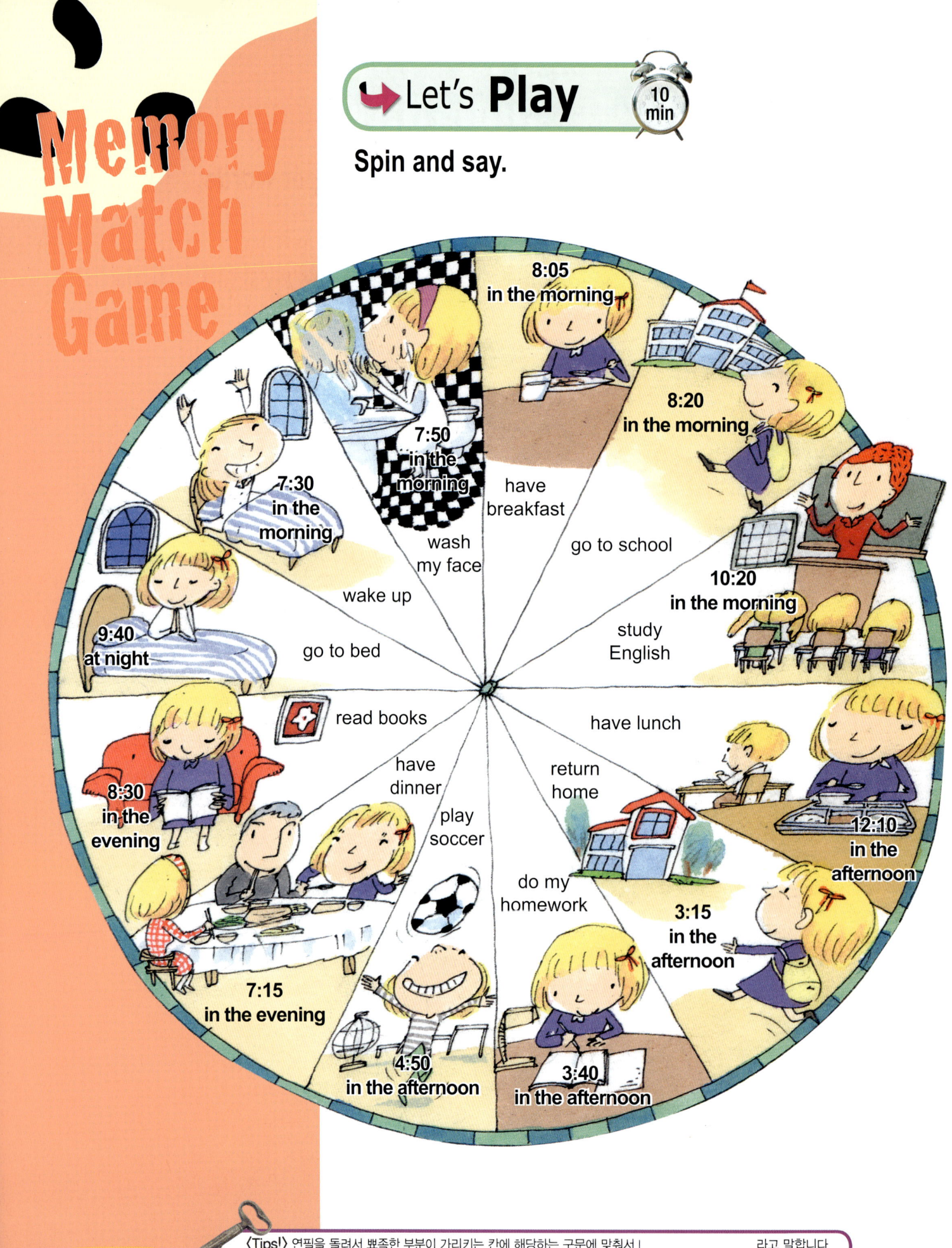

8:05
in the morning

8:20
in the morning

have
breakfast

go to school

10:20
in the morning

study
English

have lunch

return
home

12:10
in the
afternoon

do my
homework

3:15
in the
afternoon

3:40
in the afternoon

play
soccer

4:50
in the afternoon

have
dinner

7:15
in the evening

read books

8:30
in the
evening

go to bed

9:40
at night

wake up

7:30
in the
morning

wash
my face

7:50
in the
morning

〈Tips!〉 연필을 돌려서 뾰족한 부분이 가리키는 칸에 해당하는 구문에 맞춰서 I ____ _____. 라고 말합니다
ex) I wake up at 7:30 in the morning.

Let's Do It At Home

20 1. **Listen and connect each time with the correct picture.**

ⓐ 7:50   ⓑ 8:20   ⓒ 9:50   ⓓ 12:10

2. Read and put a V or an X in each circle.

❶ I run fast.

❷ Max goes down.

❸ My grandma has breakfast with me.

3. Look at Joey's schedule. Complete the sentences.

8:35	11:10	3:30	5:55	7:20
go to school	study English	play soccer	watch TV	take a shower

1. At eight thirty five,
   I _____.

2. At five fifty five,
   I _____.

3. At eleven ten,
   I _____.

I Go To Church Every Sunday

DATE /

❶

Bob: Joey, we have a soccer match this Sunday. Can you join us?

Joey: Oh, I'm sorry. I go to church and visit my grandparents on Sundays.

❷

Bob: Do you visit your grandparents?

Joey: Yes. After church, my grandma always cooks for my family.

☺ Role play

What do you do on Sundays?

I go to church on Sundays.

play the piano on Mondays

paint on Tuesdays

❸

Bob: Then, how about this Wednesday?

Joey: Wednesday? I have a science class after school on Wednesdays.

Bob: What do you learn?

❹

Joey: Right now we are making our own robots.

Bob: Wow, a robot? Can I come with you?

❺

Joey: Sure! But what about the soccer match?

Bob: Hmm... I don't know! But I love robots!

water the plants on Wednesdays

take a ballet lesson on Thursdays

go to the library and read books on Fridays

go hiking on Saturdays

❀ Let's Practice

 22 Listen and choose the correct person.

❶   ❷   ❸

A   B   A   B   A   B

⊚ Sight Word Zone!

 23 Listen and repeat.

my	me	up
	on	off	jump

Let's trace and write.

my my my my

me me me me

up up up up

on on on on

off off off off

jump jump jump jump

Check & Check

15 min

24 **Listen and fill in the blanks.**

> Don't _____ _____ my bed!

> Get _____ of _____ room.

> Help me!

> Watch _____ ! You are about to step ____ the broken glass!

> You saved _____. Thank you very much.

① ② ③ ④

Solve the ladder puzzle and write.

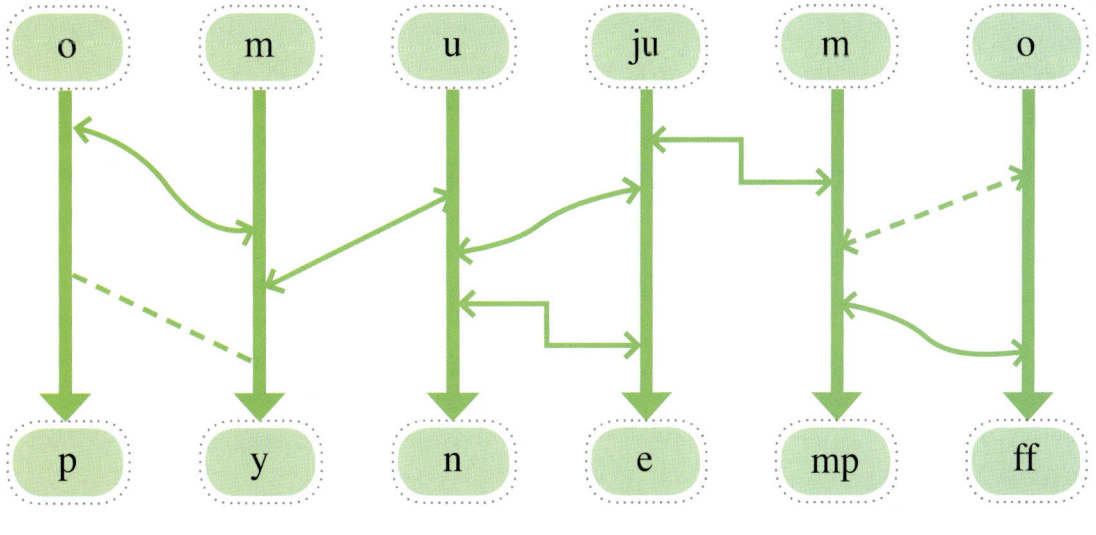

o	m	u	ju	m	o
p	y	n	e	mp	ff

_____ _____ _____ _____ _____ _____

Coin Soccer!

Let's Play

15 min

You Need
a coin

Let's play a soccer game!

2pts
go hiking

3pts

2pts
go the the library

1pt
play soccer

1pt
water plant

1pt
go to church

1pt
play the piano

1pt
paint

1pt
visit my grandparents

1pt
play baseball

1pt
read books

2pts
take a ballet class

3pts

2pts
make cookies

My Goal Card

My Goal Card

〈Tips!〉 ❶ 축구장 보드 위에서 동전들을 손가락으로 튕겨서 만난 단어 축구공의 표현들을 이용하여 문장을 만듭니다. 그리고 아래의 'Ball Card'에 그 표현을 써서 카드를 채웁니다.
❷ 자신이 만난 표현을 말하거나 또는 그 표현을 이용해 문장을 말하면 그 단어의 점수를 얻습니다.
또 상대의 골대에 동전을 넣어도 3points 점수를 얻습니다.
❸ My Goal Card를 다 채우면 게임을 끝내고 점수를 계산합니다.
❹ 가장 높은 점수를 얻은 사람이 승리!

Score Board

Let's Do It At Home

1. Listen and circle.

①   A   B   ②   A   B

2. Unscramble the sentences.

① cooks / My / me / Sunday / every / grandma / . / for

_____

② ballet / . / I / lesson / on / a / take / Thursdays

_____

③ he / What / do / on / does / ? / Saturdays

_____

3. Choose the right words and complete the sentences.

Let _____ my/me introduce _____ my/me family.

The man _____ on/off the ladder is _____ my/me dad.

The lady turning _____ off/up the lamp is

_____ my/me mom. _____ My/Me brother is

_____ run/jump ing.

_____ My/Me sister is going _____ on/up the stairs.

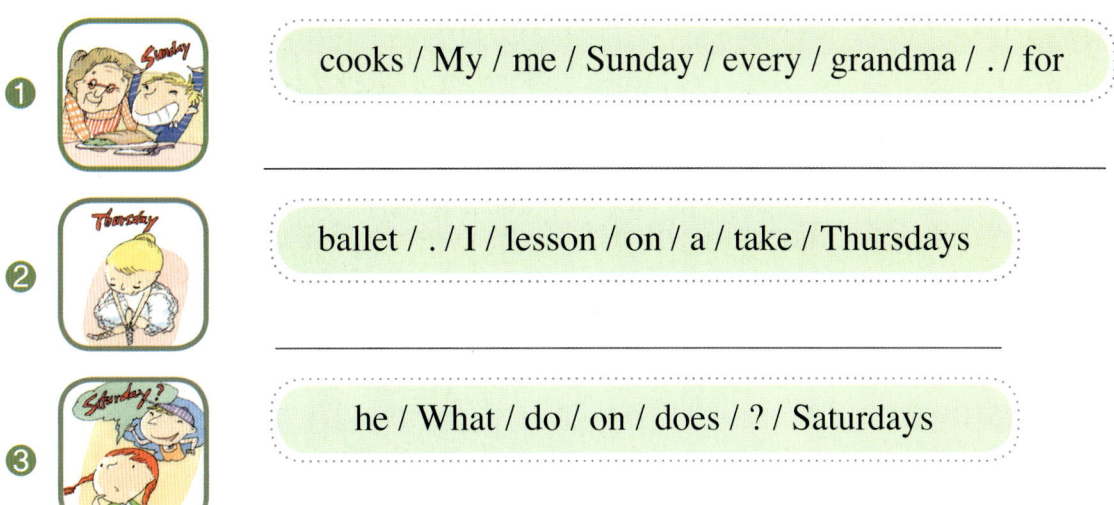

Unit 6 I Like Sunny Days

DATE /

①

Mike: Mom, it's raining outside.

Mom: It is thundering, too.

Mike: I'm scared. I don't like rainy days.

Mom: What kind of weather do you like?

Mike: I like sunny days because I can swim in the warm sunlight.

😊 Role play

What kind of weather do you like?

I like sunny days because I can swim in the warm sunlight.

windy days
fly a kite

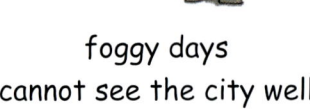

foggy days
cannot see the city well

❷

Mom: That's great. I also like sunny days, but I like the thunder, too.

Mike: Interesting. Why?

Mom: When the sky catches a cold, it coughs.

Mike: Really?

Mom: Yes. The cough sound is the thundering. I'm not afraid of thunder.

Mike: Now I'm not afraid either! (Roaring) It really docs sound like a cough!

stormy days
play board games with my family

cloudy days
walk outside

rainy days
hear frogs crying

snowy days
make a snowman

 27 Listen and number in order.

Sight Word Zone!

 28 Listen and repeat.

> went   had   good
>
> stop   get   got

Let's trace and write.

went went went went

had had had had

good good good good

stop stop stop stop

get get get get

got got got got

Check & Check

29 **Listen and fill in the blanks by choosing the proper words.**

❶ I _____ want/went to the bus _____ stop/shop last night.

❷ I _____ get/got up at 8:30 this morning. I'm late for school!

❸ My friend Joe is very _____ got/good at Math. She always _____ get/got s good grades.

Find the words in the puzzle.

went
had
get
got
good
stop

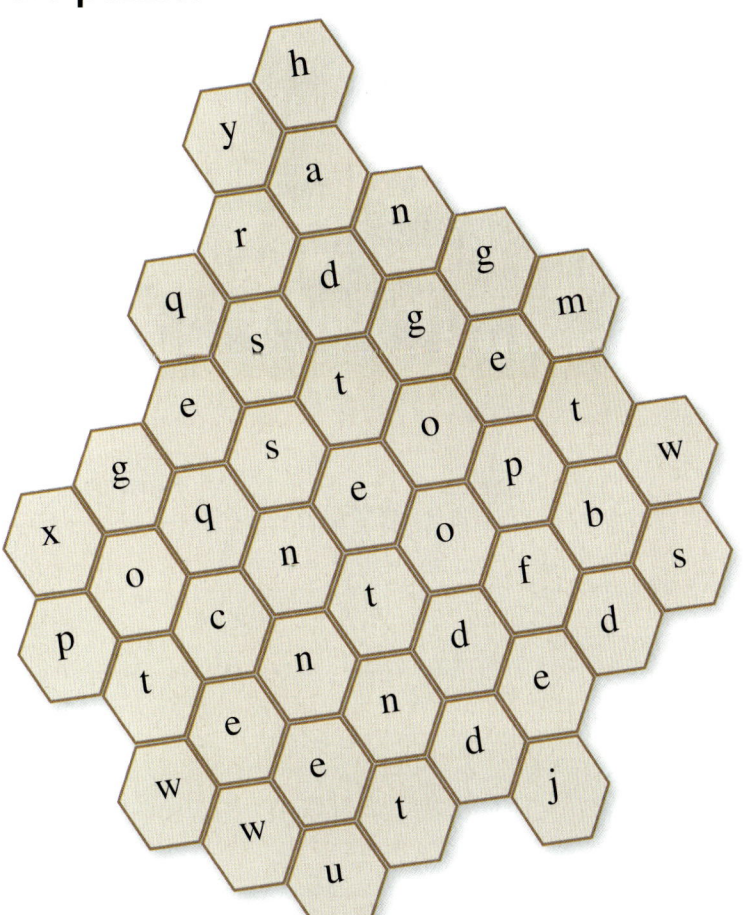

Weather Diary

Let's **Play**

15 min

Cut and paste.

You Need ✂ scissors   🗜 stapler   ✏ pencil

My Weather Diary

NAME

In sunny days…   In snowy days…

In rainy days…   In windy days…

〈Tips!〉 각각을 잘라내어 속지에는 각 날씨에 관련된 활동이나 자신의 이야기를 생각하며 쓰고 바깥접기를 해서 맨 위의 겉장에 삽입하여 스테이플러로 고정합니다. 그러면 My Weather Diary 완성!

Let's Do It At Home

 1. Listen and place the word stickers correctly. Sticker

①  ②  ③

④  ⑤  ⑥

2. Read and match.

① I like snowy days because I can make a snowman.

② I like rainy days because I can hear the frogs cry.

③ I like cloudy days because I can walk outside.

ⓐ

ⓑ

ⓒ

3. Unscramble the sentences.

① do / like / ? / weather / you / What kind of

_____

② can /sunny /. / swim / days / I / on

_____

Unit 7

The Months June, July And August Are In The Summer

❶

Max: When is your birthday, Tina?

Tina: My birthday is August 28th.

 **Role play**

The months June, July and August are in the summer.

❷

Max: Is that in the fall?

Tina: No, it's in the summer. The months June, July and August are in the summer. I like summer.

Max: You do? I don't. Summer is too hot!

March, April, and May / spring

September, October, and November / fall

December, January, and February / winter

❸ Tina: But I can swim at the beach in the summer!

Max: Yeah. But the sun in the summer is too hot.

❹

Tina: But my birthday is in the summer!

Max: OK. OK. I like summer, too...

Spring is warm.
I can go on a picnic
in spring.

summer
hot and sunny
swim at the beach

fall
cool and windy
fly a kite

winter
cold and snowy
go skiing

❀ Let's Practice

 32 **Listen and choose the correct picture.**

①   A   B   ②   A   B   ③   A

B

🌀 Sight Word Zone!

 33 **Listen and repeat.**

> do   did   don't
>
> and   father   friend

Let's trace and write.

do do do do

did did did did

don't don't don't don't

and and and and

father father father father

friend friend friend friend

Check & Check

 15 min

 Listen and fill in the blanks by choosing the proper words.

❶ My _____ mother's/father's birthday is in November,
_____ and/in my _____ mother's/father's birthday
is in February.

❷ _____ Do/Did you know how to fly a kite?
No, I _____ don't/didn't . Let's ask my _____ mother/father .

❸ Why _____ do/did you bring cup cakes yesterday?
Because yesterday was my best _____
father's/friend's birthday.

❹ What can you _____ do/did in the winter?
I can go skiing, ice skating, _____ and/but make a snowman!

 **Check the missing words and write.**

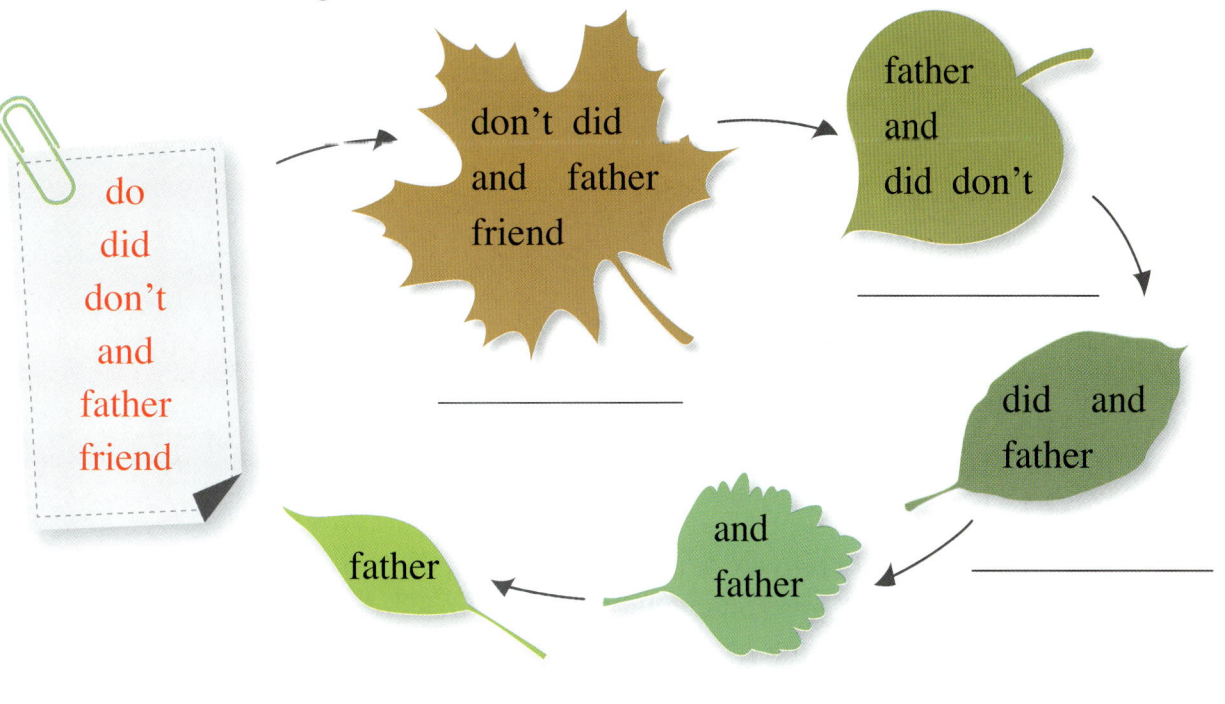

Month Puzzle

Let's **Play** 10 min

Find out the words and circle them.

C	F	U	F	L	Q	W	J	V	M	V	S	G	F	P	W
M	E	H	I	A	U	G	U	S	T	R	E	L	G	C	G
D	B	K	U	O	E	L	L	B	D	A	P	R	I	L	F
F	R	J	Y	S	M	A	Y	N	B	B	T	O	J	A	T
A	U	K	J	A	A	H	V	N	O	V	E	M	B	E	R
J	A	N	U	A	R	Y	C	L	P	O	M	B	W	A	Y
U	R	L	N	J	C	G	O	C	T	O	B	E	R	F	M
D	Y	P	E	L	H	P	X	I	C	I	E	B	E	R	U
X	W	Q	K	R	Y	T	I	N	M	R	R	E	Y	F	C
D	E	C	E	M	B	E	R	O	P	F	C	R	K	L	M

 **Let's Sing Together!**

What months are in the spring?
The months March, April and May are in the spring.
In spring I can go for a picnic.

What months are in the summer?
The months June, July and August are in the summer.
In summer I can swim, dive, and splash!

What months are in the fall?
The months September, October and November are in the fall.
In fall I can fly a kite.

What months are in the winter?
The months December, January and February are in the winter.
In winter I can go skiing. Yee-ha!

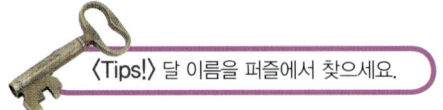 〈Tips!〉달 이름을 퍼즐에서 찾으세요.

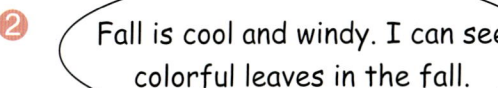

Let's Do It At Home

1. Read and write the correct number to match.

①
Winter is cold. I can make a snowman in winter.

② Fall is cool and windy. I can see colorful leaves in the fall.

Summer is hot and sunny. I can go to the beach.

③
Spring is warm. I can go on a picnic in spring.

④

2. Listen and write the words.

 36

① _____ you speak Chinese?
No, I _____.
_____ you speak English?
Yes, I _____.

② What _____ you do during the holiday?
I went on a picnic with my _____ and played computer games with my _____.

3. Write the words in the puzzle.

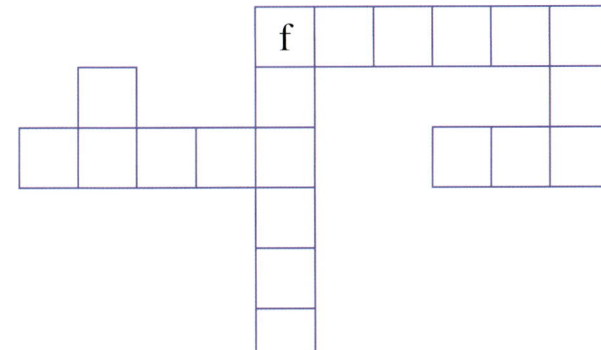

f

do
did
don't
and
father
friend

37

pets

lizard

❶

❷

Ms. Masey: We are talking about pets today. What kind of pet do you want to have, Megan?

Megan: I want to have a lizard. I know lots of things about lizards.

Ms. Masey: Really? Where do lizards live?

Megan: They live in the desert.

 Where do polar bears live?

 They live in the snow.

frogs
in a pond

bats
in a cave

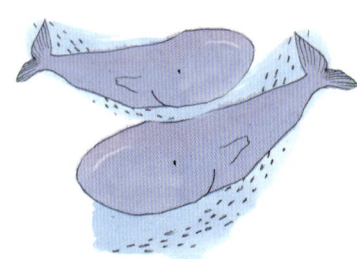

whales
in the ocean

3

Ms. Masey: Can you make a lizard tank?

Megan: Sure! I take a box and pour sand in the box. Then I can heat the room.

Ms. Masey: Wow! That's wonderful!

4

Ms. Masey: Dan, which pet do you want to have?

Dan: I want to have a pet that lives in the ocean.

Ms. Masey: The Ocean? What pet lives in the ocean?

Dan: Whales!

 Who lives in the forest?

 Skunks live in the forest.

in grassy fields
sheep

in the desert
camels

in the city
pigeons

Let's Practice

 38 Listen. If it's correct, write **O**. If it's not, write **X**.

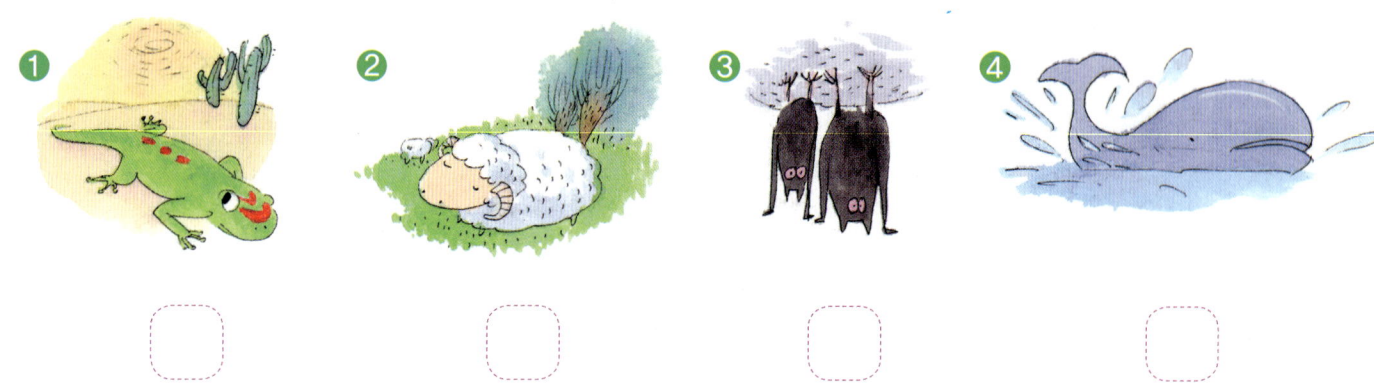

① ② ③ ④

Sight Word Zone!

 39 Listen and repeat.

in   out   ran

play   one   two

Let's trace and write.

in in in in

out out out out

ran ran ran ran

play play play play

one one one one

two two two two

Check & Check

15 min

 40

Listen and fill in the blanks.

1. Last night I ☐☐ of my room because I saw a big spider ☐ my room.

2. Today in the morning Jeff ☐ to school to ☐ with his friends.

3. I have ☐ backpack and ☐ pencil cases.

4. ☐ my classroom, there are ☐ plants; ☐ is a beanstalk,

   and the other ☐ is rosebush.

5. Please give me ☐ more glass of water. I ☐ here, so I'm very hot.

WORD BOX   one ran one two one ran ran two In one in play out

Connect the word dominoes together and write them below.

Start   on

an   pl

o   r

t   tw

n   ou

e   i

ay   Finish

Word Domino

☐—☐—☐—☐—☐

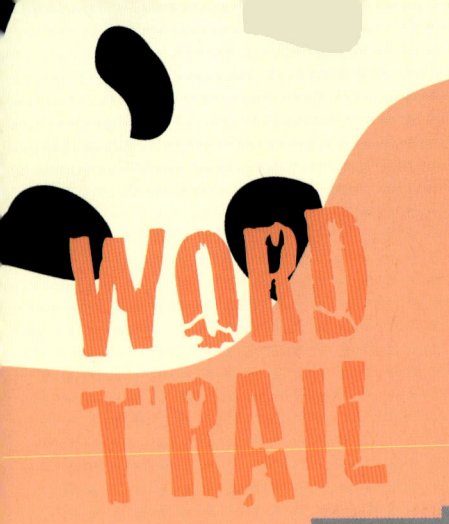

↳ Let's **Play** 🕐 15 min

Where do they live?

Use the picture clues to fill in the word trail. After finishing the WORD TRAIL, talk about the picture.

Hint

ocean
pond
cave
grassy fields
city
snow
forest
desert

⟨Tips!⟩ 그림을 보고 각 동물들이 사는 곳을 Word Trail에 채워 넣습니다. 그리고 그림을 보며 말해 보세요.
A: Where do whales live? B: They live in the ocean.

Let's Do It At Home

41

1. Listen and connect the correct words.

① ② ③ ④

ⓐ camels   ⓑ Polar bears   ⓒ grassy fields   ⓓ forest

2. Read and put a V or an X in each circle.

①   ②   ③

I go into my house.   I run and play with my dog.   It's one o'clock.

3. Look at the table. Complete the sentences.

skunks	a polar bear	whales	frogs	lizards
forest	snow	ocean	pond	desert

1. _____ in the ocean .

2. _____ in a pond .

3. _____ in the desert .

Unit 9 I Live In Italy

1 Mike: Hi, Sue. This is the second time chatting with you on the Internet.

Sue: Yes. Happy to chat with you again.

Mike: Where do you live?

Sue: I live in Italy.

Mike: Where is Italy?

Sue: Italy is in Europe.

☺ Role play

I live in Korea.
Korea is in Asia.
This is the Korean flag.

the USA
America
American

the UK
Europe
English

Canada
America
Canadian

❷

Mike: I want to go there someday.

Sue: Yes, visit Italy for a vacation.

Mike: We can watch a football game together!

Sue: Right. This is the Italian flag.

You will see the flag on the football field.

Mike: I can't wait!

Australia
Oceania
Australian

China
Asia
Chinese

Japan
Asia
Japanese

France
Europe
French

Ethiopia
Africa
Ethiopian

Let's Practice

 43 Listen and choose the correct flag.

❶	❷	❸
A B	A B	A B

Sight Word Zone!

 44 Listen and repeat.

> yes   no   you
>
> we   they   are

Let's trace and write.

yes yes yes yes

no no no no

you you you you

we we we we

they they they they

are are are are

Check & Check

 15 min

45 Listen and fill in the blanks.

Where are we going?

Look! Over there_____ some soldiers!

_____ _____ going to the UK.

OK. Let's go.

① ② ③ ④

Can _____ go into the palace?

Can we fly over the palace?

No, you cannot.

_____, _____ cannot!

Read the word reflection in the mirror and write it in correctly.

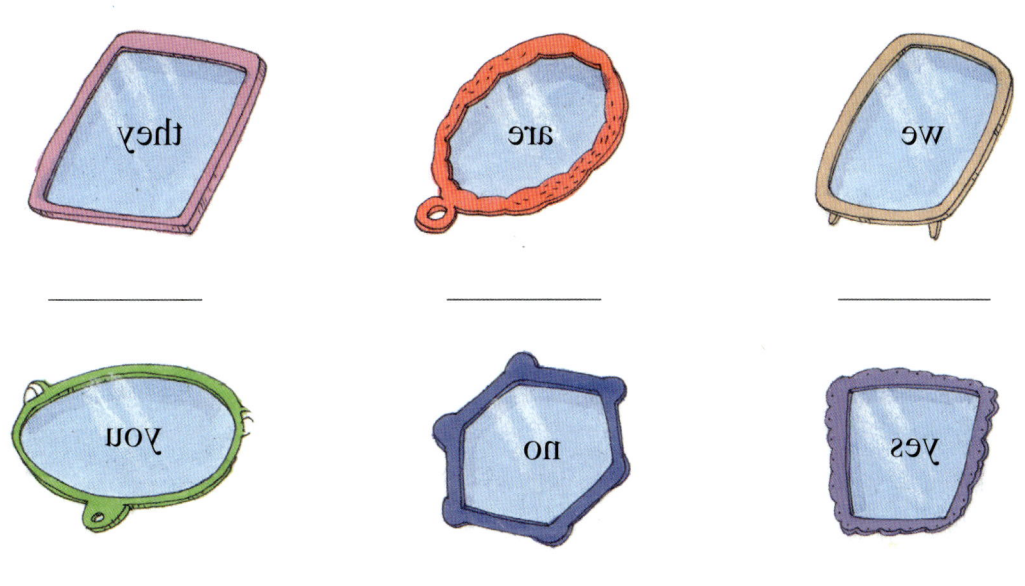

they

are

we

_____

_____

_____

you

no

yes

_____

_____

_____

Whispering!

Let's **Play**

10 min

You Need

scissors

I live in the USA. The USA is in North America.

I live in Korea. Korea is in Asia.

I live in China. China is in Asia.

I live in Ethiopia. Ethiopia is in Africa.

I live in Greece. This is the Greek flag.

I live in France. This is the French flag.

I live in the UK. This is the British flag.

I live in the USA. The USA is in North America.

I live in Korea. Korea is in Asia.

I live in China. China is in Asia.

I live in Ethiopia. Ethiopia is in Africa.

I live in Greece. This is the Greek flag.

I live in France. This is the French flag.

I live in the UK. This is the British flag.

〈Tips!〉 글자를 따라서 문장을 쓰고 선을 따라 문장을 자릅니다. Team Green 과 Team Orange를 나누어 각각 일렬로 섭니다. 줄 끝에 잘라놓은 문장 스트립을 놓습니다. 출제자가 문장을 하나 뽑아 귓속말로 전달하고 먼저 문장 스트립을 찾아내는 팀이 승리합니다.

Let's Do It At Home

46

1. Listen and circle.

①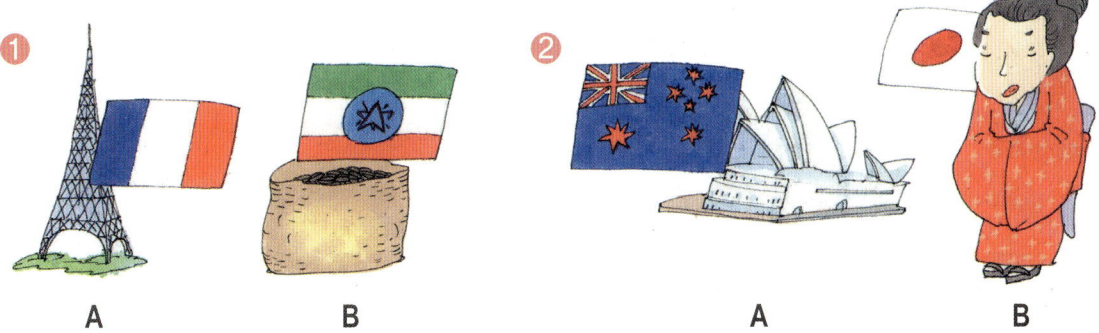

A   B   A   B

2. Unscramble the sentences and match them to the correct flags.

① •   • ⓐ   is / . / American / This / flag / the

_____

② •   • ⓑ   I / . / China / in / Asia / in / live / China / . / is

_____

③ •   • ⓒ   is / flag / the / . / Italian / This

_____

3. Choose the right words and complete the sentences.

Mike: Hi, Joshua. Can _____ we/you tell me about your country?

Joshua: _____ Yes/No . My family lives in Korea.

_____ We/They _____ is/are Koreans.

On New Year's Day _____

we/they put on traditional clothes.

Mike: That's great!

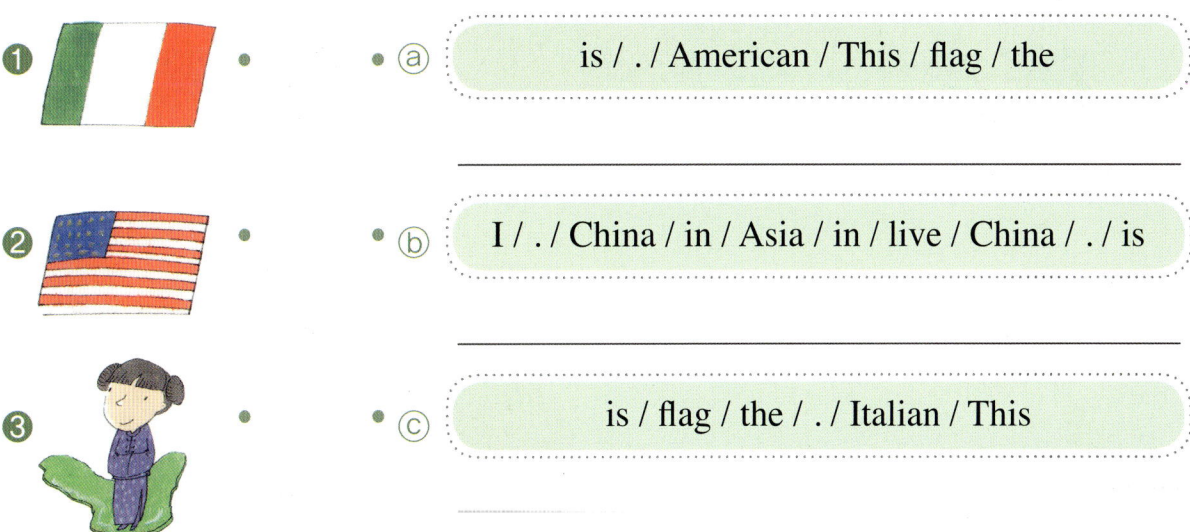

I Have A Sandwich And Orange Juice For Lunch

15 min

DATE   /

1

Bob: Oh, I'm hungry.

Tina: What are you having for lunch?

Bob: I have a sandwich and orange juice everyday, but I lost my sandwich today.

2

Tina: Oh, sorry. Then let's share my hamburger.

Bob: Thank you.

Role play

What do you eat for breakfast?

I eat scrambled eggs, bacon and milk for breakfast.

sandwich and orange juice lunch

chicken and fruit dinner

❸

Max: Bob, is this your sandwich? I found it in the play ground.

Bob: Ah, yes. That's my sandwich. Thank you very much.

❹

Bob: Now we can share my sandwich, together!

Tina: Oh, you really want this?

cereal, milk and fruit
breakfast

spaghetti and soup
lunch

steak, salad and pie
dinner

Let's Practice

 Listen and number in order.

Sight Word Zone!

 Listen and repeat.

not	ate	be
	day	three	four

Let's trace and write.

not not not not

ate ate ate ate

be be be be

day day day day

three three three three

four four four four

Check & Check

15 min

 Listen and fill in the blanks.

1. I ⬚ only one meal in the last two days.

2. ⬚ nice. Do ⬚ run in the classroom.

3. Joey ⬚ ⬚ cookies yesterday and ⬚ cookies today.

 He will ⬚ fat.

4. It's December twenty first. Christmas ⬚ is coming.

5. Do your homework first, and do ⬚ watch TV now.

WORD BOX   ate   not   day   be   not   ate   three   four   Be

Follow the lines to connect each letter cluster. Then write.

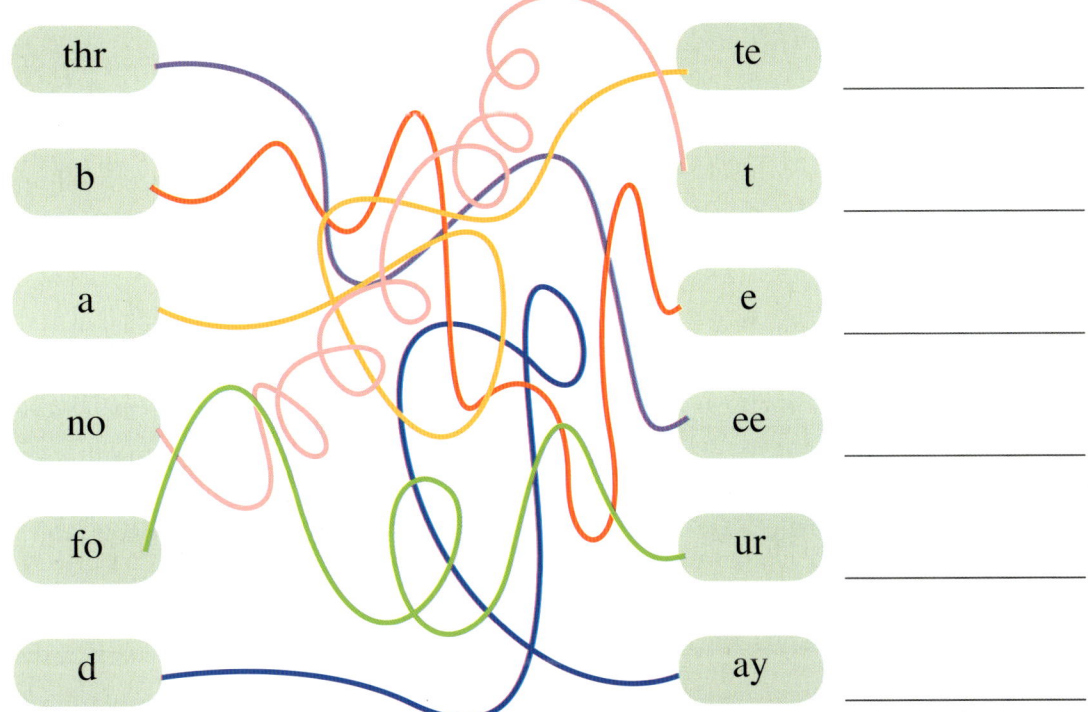

thr		te	_____
b		t	_____
a		e	_____
no		ee	_____
fo		ur	_____
d		ay	_____

You Need
scissors glue crayon

What do you eat for breakfast?

ex)

a sandwich
and orange juice

name: _____   name: _____   name: _____   name: _____

  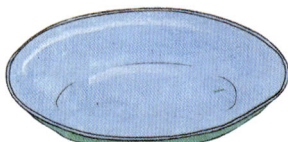

_____ eats   _____ eats   _____ eats   _____ eats

_____   _____   _____   _____

for _____.   for _____.   for _____.   for _____.

〈Tips!〉 자름 선에 따라 자르고 바르게 접어 Accordion book을 만든 뒤, 앞에 세 칸에는 내가 먹는 식사에 대해서 그림을 그리고 내용을 써 봅니다. 뒤 네 칸에는 친구들이 먹는 식사에 대해서 조사하고 써 봅니다.

Let's Do It At Home

51 **1. Listen and place the word stickers correctly.**

①  ②  ③

④  ⑤  ⑥

2. Read and match.

① I eat hamburger and grape juice for lunch. •   • ⓐ

② I eat chicken and salad for dinner. •   • ⓑ

③ I eat milk and toast for breakfast. •   • ⓒ

3. Unscramble the sentences.

① do / breakfast / What / ? / for / you / eat

_____

② eat / and / dinner / salad / I / . / steak / for

_____

Unit 11 It Tastes Sweet

DATE   /

❶ Tina: Do you like chocolate cake, Max?

Max: Yes, I do.

Tina: I have some chocolate cake for you.

Max: Thank you very much!

❷ Tina: How does it taste?

Max: It tastes sweet. I love it!

😊 Role play

Do you like bacon?

Yes, I do.

How does it taste?

It tastes salty and greasy.

French fries
greasy

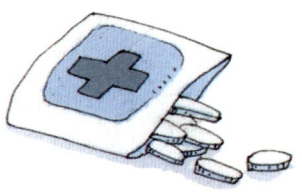

medicine
bitter

❸ Max: Heart, I have some chocolate cake for you.

Heart: Thank you very much.

❹ Max: What does it taste like?

Heart: It tastes bitter.

Max: Oh, my! I forgot the sugar! I'm sorry!

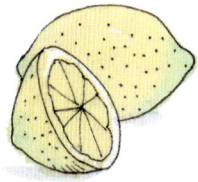

lemon
sour

red pepper
hot

cookies
sweet

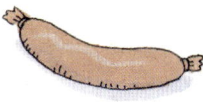

sausage
salty

Let's Practice

 53 **Listen and choose the correct tastes.**

1
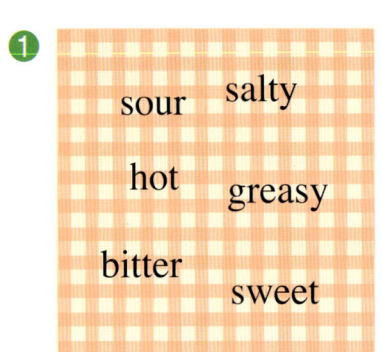

sour salty

hot greasy

bitter

sweet

2

sweet

sour

salty

greasy

hot

bitter

3
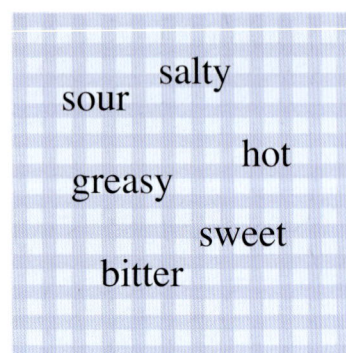

salty

sour

hot

greasy

sweet

bitter

Sight Word Zone!

 54 **Listen and repeat.**

of	sit	sat
look	night	rain

Let's trace and write.

of of of of

sit sit sit sit

sat sat sat sat

look look look look

night night night night

rain rain rain rain

Check & Check

15 min

 55 **Listen and fill in the blanks by choosing the proper words.**

❶ What happened to you? You _____ rain/look sick.

❷ I _____ sit/sat on a bench last _____ night/rain ,
when it suddenly _____ snow/rain ed.

❸ Let's _____ sit/sat and _____ look/rain
at the blue sky. It's so beautiful!

❹ I bought a new book last _____ sat/night .
The title _____ off/of the book is "The adventures
_____ on/of Tom Sawyer."

Find the words from each letter soup and write them in.

sejofgwenuiklc

puibgtussrainw

nightiawxfhhs

_____

_____

_____

yttxcrtleomssit

mnfxsyrsjglook

hnhiyrsatyimkop

_____

_____

_____

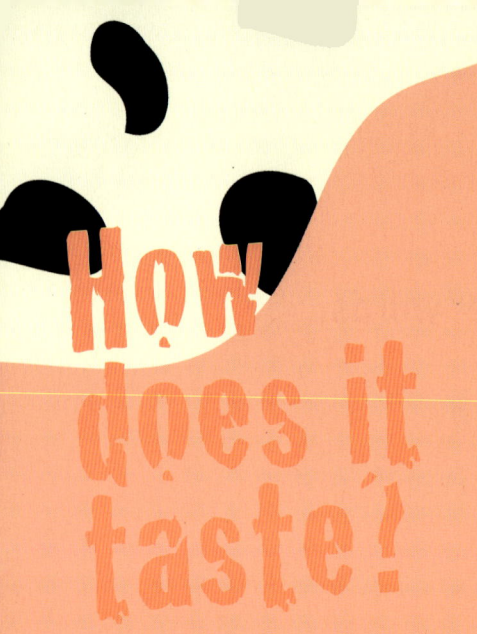

How does it taste?

Fill in the blanks correctly and draw the proper facial expressions.

| sour | salty | sweet |
| hot | greasy | bitter |

I have medicine.
It tastes _____.

I have red pepper.
It tastes _____.

I have bacon.
It tastes _____.

I have lemon.
It tastes _____.

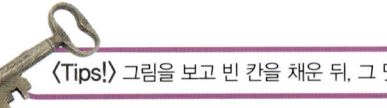
〈Tips!〉 그림을 보고 빈 칸을 채운 뒤, 그 맛에 어울리게 얼굴 표정을 그려보세요.

Let's Do It At Home

1. Read and write the correct number to match.

① I'm Pam. I like cola. It tastes bitter but sweet.

② I'm Megan. I like salsa and tortilla chips. It's hot and spicy.

③ I'm Max. I like fried fish. It tastes greasy and salty.

④ I'm Alice. I caught a cold and I am taking medicine. It tastes bitter.

 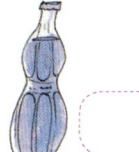  

2. Listen and write the words.

① _____ up straight in class.
_____ at the board carefully.

② Last _____, it rained a lot.
Most _____ the trees in town fell down because of the _____.

3. Write the words in the puzzle.

a

t

s   t

salty
bitter
sit
sat
rain
night
sour

15 min

57

Unit 12

I Want To Swim At The Swimming Pool

DATE /

 1

Alice: Joey, I want to go swimming. Where can I swim?

Joey: You can swim at the swimming pool.

There is a new swimming pool on Queen's Road.

Alice: I want to go there now!

Joey: Now? Do you have a swim suit?

😊 Role play

A: I want to buy a book. Where can I buy one?

B: You can buy a book at the bookstore. It's on King's Road.

to buy some flowers
flower shop

to watch a movie
theater

❷

Alice: No, I don't. I should buy a swim suit.
　　　　Where can I buy one?

Joey: You can buy one at the department store.
　　　　It's on Apple Street.

Alice: Okay. Let's go to the department store!

Joey: Alright. Let's go!

to have my hair cut
beauty salon

to mail a letter
post office

to buy some vegetables
grocery store

✿Let's Practice

 58 Listen. If the picture is correct, write **O**. But if not, then write **X**.

① ② ③ ④

⑥Sight Word Zone!

 59 Listen and repeat.

eat	for	if
	from	five	six

Let's trace and write.

eat eat eat eat

for for for for

if if if if

from from from from

five five five five

six six six six

 60 **Listen and circle the correct words for each sentence.**

❶ _____ At/If you want to _____ eat/ate dinner with us, please come back early.

❷ I brought a story book _____ from/for school. I will read it _____ from/for my grandma.

❸ My friend Alice sent me _____ five/four dolls from the USA. She bought them _____ for/from me.

🍬 **Trace each letter and make words with them.**

_____   _____   _____

_____   _____   _____

Let's **Play**

 15 min

You Need — coins pencil scissors

Spin, mark the map and say.

the grocery store   the department store   the hair salon   the pharmacy

the toy store   the flower shop   the theater   the book store

buy some books

buy a swim suit

watch a movie

buy medicine

buy toys

buy some flowers

have my hair cut

buy some vegetables

〈Tips!〉 연필을 돌려서 뾰족한 부분이 가리키는 칸에 해당하는 구문에 맞춰서 I want to _____. 라고 말합니다. 그러면 다른 친구들이나 선생님은 "Where can you buy ____?" 라고 질문해 주세요. 게임을 하는 사람은 자신의 동전을 관련된 장소에 놓고 I can buy _____ at _____. 라고 말합니다.

Let's Do It At Home

61

1. Listen and connect each place with the correct picture.

ⓐ book store   ⓑ post office   ⓒ swimming pool   ⓓ flower shop

2. Read and put a V or an X.

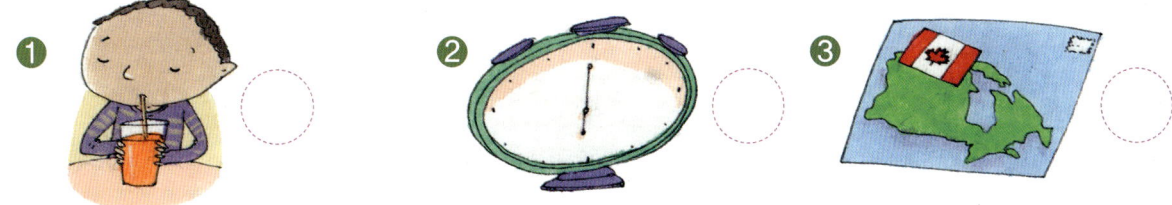

❶ He's eating peanuts.   ❷ It's five to six.   ❸ This postcard is from Canada.

3. Look at Joey's schedule. Complete the sentences.

beauty salon	post office	grocery store	bookstore	theater
have my hair cut	mail a letter	buy some vegetables	buy a book	see a movie

1. At the grocery store,
   I want to _____.

2. At the post office,
   I want to _____.

3. At the theater,
   I want to _____.

Unit 13 I Want To Ride The Merry-Go-Round

DATE /

Sue: We're at the amusement park!
Neo: I'm so excited!

Sue: I want to ride the merry-go-round.
Neo: Yes, I want to also.

😊 Role play

I want to ride the merry-go-round.

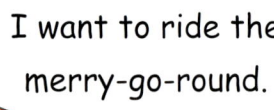

Sue: I want to ride the roller coaster.
Neo: Oh, no! I don't like heights. I don't want to. Ugh!

miniature railway

log flume

spinning cups

roller coaster

❸

Sue: I want to ride the bumper car.

This is really exciting.

Neo: Watch out!

❹

Sue: I want to ride the spinning cups!

Neo: I feel dizzy.

❻

Sue: Now, I want to ride the ferries wheel.

Neo: I want to go home and sleep.

motion simulator

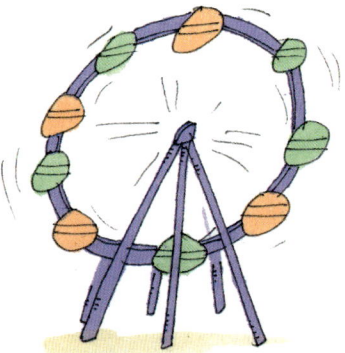

ferries wheel

pirate ship

bumper car

Let's Practice

63 **Listen and choose the right person.**

① A   B   ② A   B   ③ A   B

Sight Word Zone!

64 **Listen and repeat.**

can	car	book
go	new	green

Let's trace and write.

can can can can

car car car car

book book book book

go go go go

new new new new

green green green green

Check & Check

15 min

65 **Listen and fill in the blanks.**

How _____ we _____ into the palace?

Hmm. I have no idea.

What's that over there?
It's a _____ _____ .

Whose is that?

Oh, it's my _____ !
Thank you very much!

Are you busy now? I want to invite you to my house.
My _____ is nearby.

You're welcome!

We'd love to. Thank you!

Solve the ladder puzzle and write.

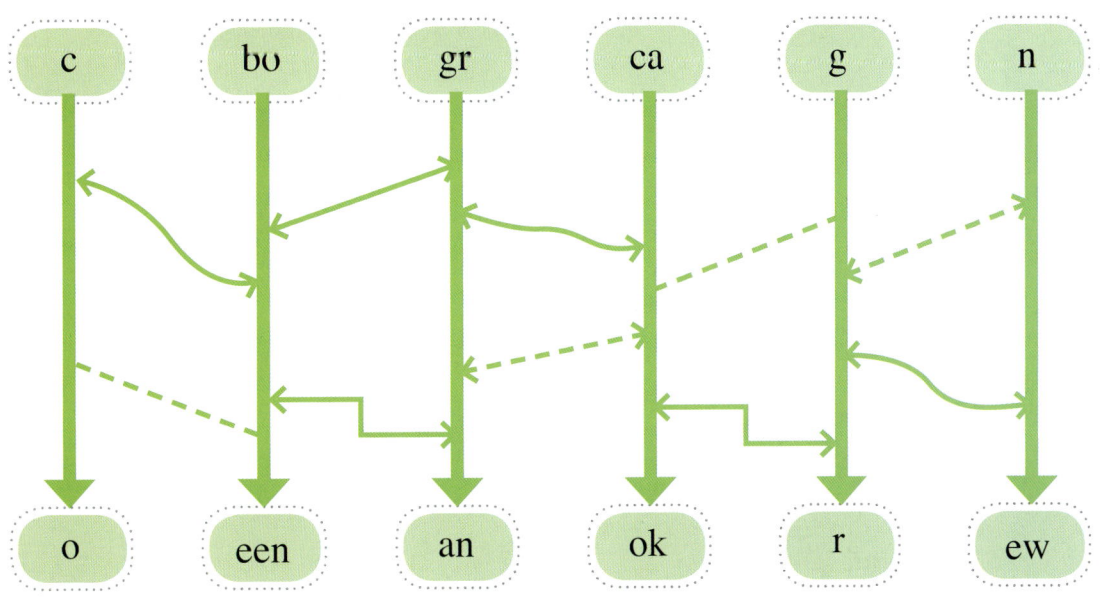

c	bo	gr	ca	g	n
o	een	an	ok	r	ew

_____ _____ _____ _____ _____

I want to ride …

You Need — a die — markers

"Resting place"

merry-go-round

+2

-1

roller coaster

log flume

-2

miniature railway

+1

bumper car

-1

FINISH!

-2

START Here!

+2

motion simulator

spinning cups

"Toilet"

ferries wheel

AMUSEMENT PARK

〈Tips!〉주사위를 굴려서 숫자만큼 말을 이동하여 칸에 해당하는 단어를 사용하여 놀이공원에서 타고싶은 기구를 말합니다. "Toilet"에서는 한 번 쉬고 "Resting Place"에서는 원하는 팀의 말과 자리를 바꿉니다.

Let's Do It At Home

66

1. Listen and circle.

①   A   B   ②   A   B

2. Unscramble the sentences.

❶   want / ride / coaster / to / a / I / . / roller

_____

❷   home / . / to / sleep / I / and / go / want

_____

❸   I / ride / ship / want / . / to / pirate / a

_____

3. Choose the correct words and fill complete the sentences.

Tomorrow my younger sister will _____ come/go to school.

Mom bought _____ old/new notebooks, pencils and a back pack

for her. Dad bought a new _____ green/grey

coat, too. I am so happy to_____ come/go

to school with her.

1

Bob: Welcome to my house.

Joey: Thank you for inviting me.

Bob: Come and let's play with some toys.

It's time for a snack!

2 Joey: Don't you clean up your room?

Bob: I like to play with toys. But I don't like to clean my room.

Joey: But…

Bob: Let's go to another room.

Role play

I like to sing, but I don't like to read books.

to play soccer
to take a bath

to paint
to play the piano

❸ Bob: Hmm! I want to have cookies, cake, and milk for a snack.

Mom: After cleaning up your room!

❹ Joey: See? You should clean up your room after playing with toys!

Bob: Oh, I don't like cleaning.

to take a science class
to dance in ballet class

to cook
to play computer games

to water the plants
to take care of my baby sister

✿ Let's Practice

68 Listen and number in order.

◎ Sight Word Zone!

69 Listen and repeat.

red   see   saw

that   seven   eight

Let's trace and write.

red red red red

see see see see

saw saw saw saw

that that that that

seven seven seven seven

eight eight eight eight

Check & Check

 Listen and fill in the blanks.

1. Do you [ ] the girl over there? Who is [ ]?

2. A girl in the [ ] coat? She's my sister Annie.

3. There were [ ] students in the classroom yesterday.

   Bob is absent today, so there are [ ] students today.

4. Last night I [ ] Alice running with her [ ]-year-old brother.

5. I was [ ] years old last year. Now I'm nine.

WORD BOX   see   eight   saw   seven   eight   red   that   seven

Connect the word dominoes together and write them below.

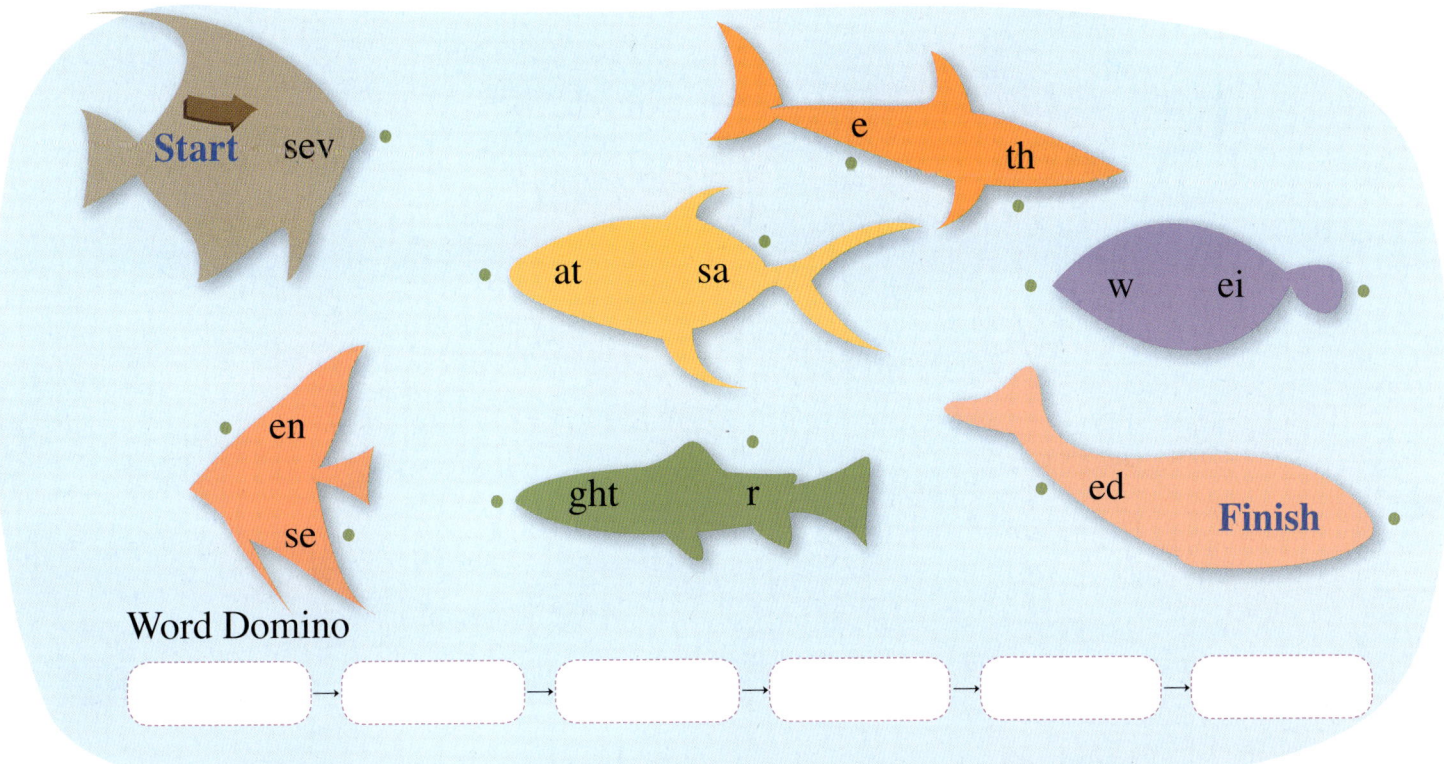

Start   sev

e   th

at   sa

w   ei

en

ght   r

ed   Finish

se

Word Domino

[ ] → [ ] → [ ] → [ ] → [ ] → [ ]

Cut and play

Let's **Play**

15 min

You Need

scissors

What do you want to do?

to sing	to go hiking	to study English	to play soccer
to dance in ballet class	to do homework	to swim in the pool	to take a science class
to water the plants	to clean up my room	to ride a roller coaster	to play the violin
to cook	to take care of my baby sister	to listen to music	to play board games

〈Tips!〉 두 명씩 한 팀이 되어 카드를 잘라 모두 뒤집어 놓고, 두 개씩 골라 뒤집어서 문장을 말합니다. 웃고 있는 모습이 담긴 그림으로는 I like to _____. 난감한 표정의 얼굴이 담긴 그림으로는 I don't like to _____. 와 같이 말해 보세요.

Let's Do It At Home

 1. Listen and place the word stickers correctly. Sticker

①    ②    ③

④    ⑤    ⑥

2. Read and match.

① I don't like to clean up my room.

② I like to sing and play the piano.

③ I like to take care of my baby sister.

 ⓐ

 ⓑ

 ⓒ

3. Unscramble the sentences.

① 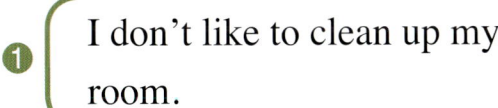 like / I / . / water / I / to /the / plants / don't

_____

② your / Don't / ? / up / you / room / clean

_____

My Leg Is Longer Than Your Leg

Unit 15

15 min

72

DATE /

Rabbit: Let's have a race.

Before the race, let's look at our bodies.

Turtle: Which is longer?

Rabbit: My leg is longer than your leg.

Role play

My ruler is longer than Sally's ruler.

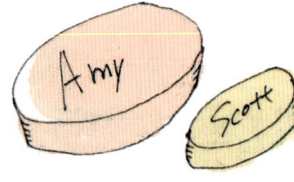

bigger   heavier   healthier

❷ Turtle: Whose eyes are bigger?

Rabbit: My eyes are bigger than your eyes.

❸

Turtle: Whose feet are smaller?

Rabbit: Your feet are smaller than my feet.

Turtle: Hmm. OK. Follow me!

❹

Turtle: But I have more brothers than you do!

higher

fatter

faster

Let's Practice

 73 Listen and choose the correct one.

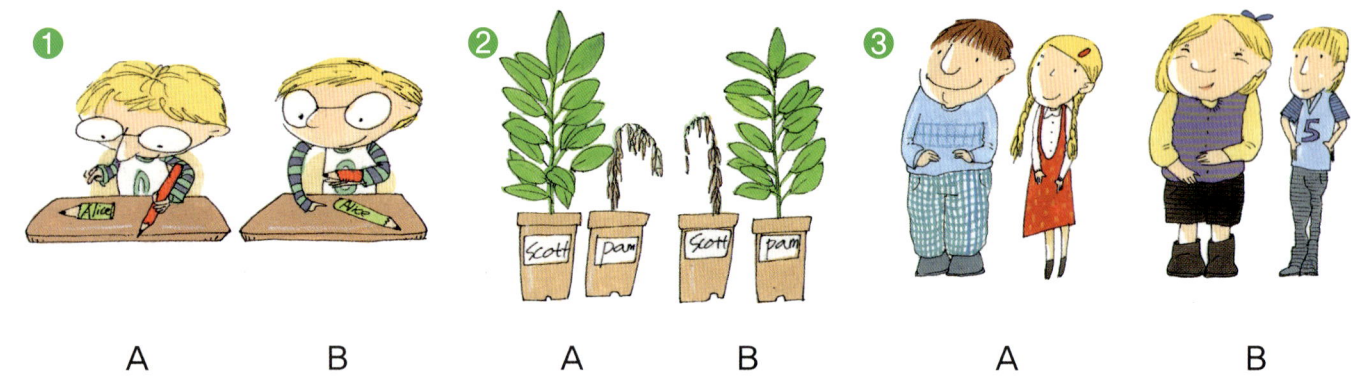

①   A   B   ②   A   B   ③   A   B

Sight Word Zone!

 74 Listen and repeat.

> this   want   yellow
>
> give   come   came

Let's trace and write.

this this this this

want want want want

yellow yellow yellow yellow

give give give give

come come come come

came came came came

Check & Check

Listen and fill in the blanks by choosing the proper words.

❶ I _____ wonder/want my friend to _____ come/came to my house.

❷ Sally asked me to pass her _____ yellow/white salt shaker.

❸ Jack _____ come/came to my house yesterday and Nicole _____ come/came s to my house today.

 Circle the words.

yellow
come
give
this
came

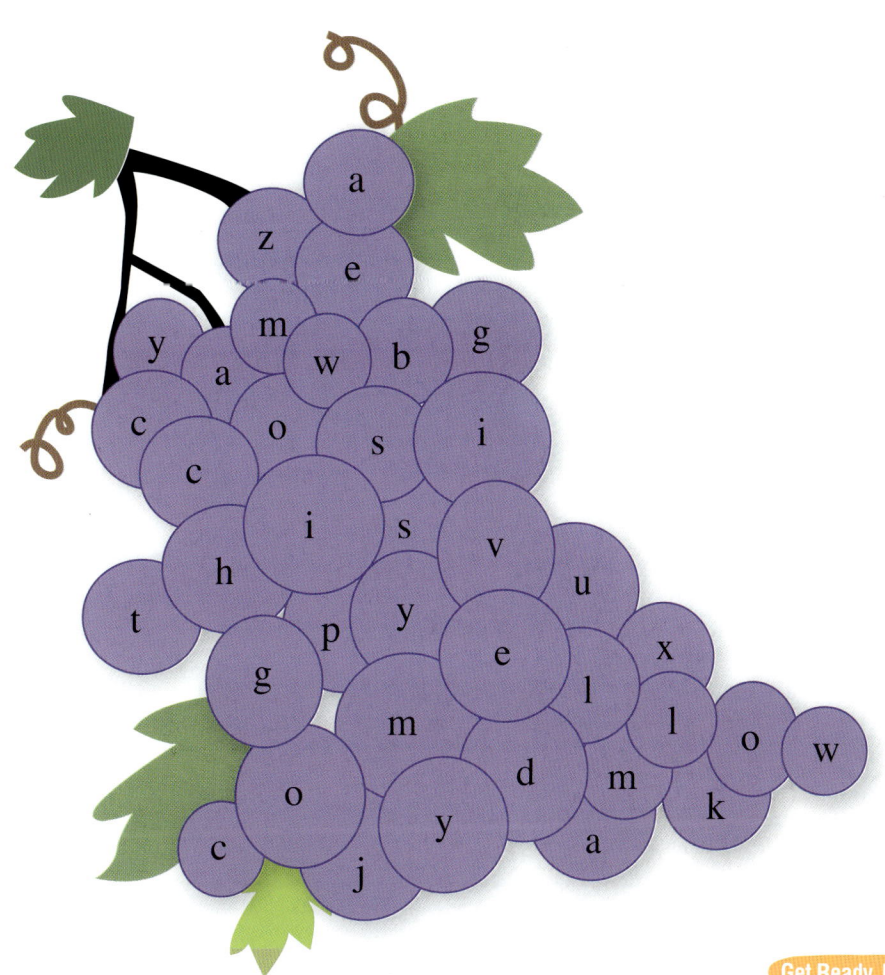

You Need scissors

Let's play Tic Tac Toe game!

heavier	sweeter	younger	longer
bigger	older	higher	taller
lighter	darker	fatter	faster
slower	shorter	smaller	healthier

〈Tips!〉 ❶ 두 사람(또는 두 팀)이 게임 순서를 정하고, 자신의 마커들을 정합니다.

❷ 게임순서에 따라서 마커들을 보드판 위에 하나씩 올려놓는데, 올려놓은 곳의 그림을 읽어야 합니다.

❸ 대각선, 가로, 또는 세로로 4칸짜리 한 줄 위에 자신의 마커를 먼저 올려 놓는 사람이 승리! (마커 대신 스티커를 사용해도 됩니다.)

Let's Do It At Home

1. Read and find the picture. If it's correct, write O. If it's not write X.

I'm Tina. My back pack is heavier than Bob's backpack.

I'm Scott. My pencil is shorter than Bob's pencil.

I'm Bob. My cell phone is smaller than Scott's cell phone.

I'm Alice. My feet are bigger than Tina's feet.

76

2. Listen and write the words.

❶ Joey _____ to my house yesterday.
You can _____ to my house today.

❷ I _____ a _____ colored pencil.
Please, _____ one to me.

3. Write the words in the puzzle.

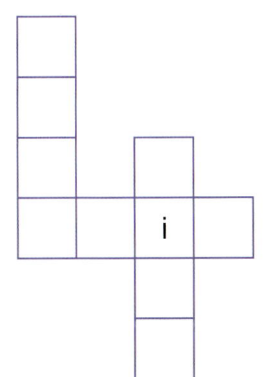
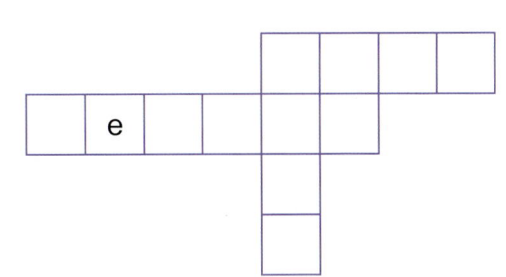

this
want
yellow
give
come
came

Unit 16
The Lion Is The Strongest Among Us

DATE /

Rabbit: Hello!

Mouse: Hello!

Fox: I'm the tallest among us!

Fox: I'm the strongest among us!

Rabbit: So, what's wrong?

Mouse: Help!

Role play

Who is the tallest here?

The giraffe is the tallest here.

the shortest/the slowest

the fastest

the strongest

❸

Lion: What's going on?

Rabbit & Fox: Please, help!

❹

Lion: Are you the strongest here?

Mouse: Fox. You're not the strongest among us, now!

Rabbit: The lion is the strongest!

Fox: Sorry! Forgive me, please!

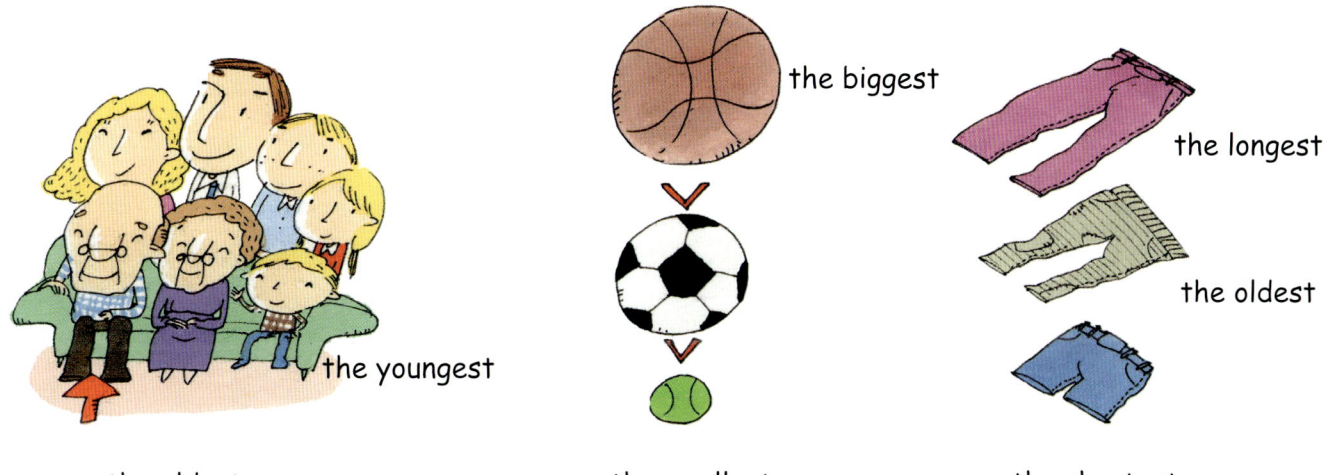

the youngest

the oldest

the biggest

the smallest

the longest

the oldest

the shortest

Let's Practice

 78 Listen. If it's correct, write **O**. If it's not, write **X**.

① ②

③ ④

Sight Word Zone!

 79 Listen and repeat.

will	old	with
blue	nine	ten

Let's trace and write.

will twill will will

old old old old

with with with with

blue blue blue blue

nine nine nine nine

ten ten ten ten

Check & Check

15 min

80 Listen and fill in the blanks.

Wow! You're the princess of this palace!

Your Majesty!

There are _____ guards following her.

Thanks for your help. These _____ ribbons are gifts for you.

Bye!

Umm... _____ you be my guard? Please, always be _____ me.

Thank you, but my _____ friends are waiting for me. See you later!

Unscramble the words then write.

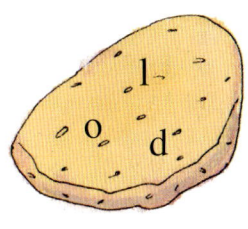

_____

_____

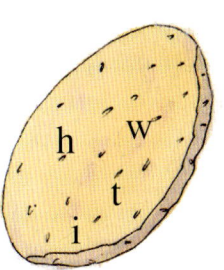

_____

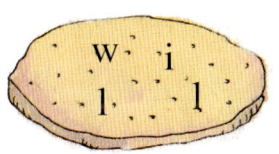

_____

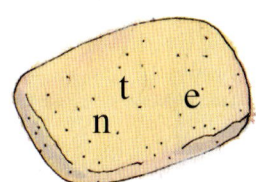

_____

_____

Use the picture clues to fill in the word trail. After finishing the WORD TRAIL, talk about the picture.

❶ ❷

❶ ❷

❸ ❹ ❸

❻

❺ ❻

❺ ❹

〈Tips!〉 그림을 보고 해당하는 단어를 Word Trail에 채웁니다. 그리고 그림에 대해 말해보세요.

Let's Do It At Home

81

1. Listen and choose the correct words for the beep sounds.

① ② ③ ④

ⓐ nine   ⓑ with   ⓒ blue   ⓓ old

2. Read and put a **V** or an **X** in each circle.

① ② ③

The tiger is the fastest. ◯

The green hat is the smallest. ◯

Bob is the youngest. ◯

3. Look at the table. Complete the sentences.

1. Who is the strongest?

   _____.

2. Who is the tallest?

   _____.

3. Who is the shortest?

   _____.

Bob   Pam   Alice   Scott   Tina

Unit 1 My Brother Mike Is Tall And Fat

check box	
parents	
teacher	

New Vocabularies

tall	tall	cute	cute
fat	fat	mother	mother
short	short	father	father
pretty	pretty	uncle	uncle
smart	smart	sister	sister
kind	kind	brother	brother
wise	wise	baby	baby
old	old	a	a
young	young	an	an
thin	thin	she	she
healthy	healthy	boy	boy
strong	strong	girl	girl
funny	funny	he	he
grandmother	grandmother		
grandfather	grandfather		

New Expressions

Who is this?

That is my brother.

He is tall and funny.

<table>
<tr><td colspan="2">check box</td></tr>
<tr><td>parents</td><td></td></tr>
<tr><td>teacher</td><td></td></tr>
</table>

Unit 2 Mom Is Cooking In The Kitchen

New Vocabularies

bedroom	bedroom	fix a car	fix a car
bathroom	bathroom	cook dinner	cook dinner
kitchen	kitchen	as	as
dining room	dining room	by	by
living room	living room	has	has
yard	yard	at	at
take a shower	take a shower		
sleep	sleep	goes	goes
read a newspaper	read a newspaper		
feed the baby	feed the baby	is	is

Express Yourself

Where is your dad?

He is in the living room.

He is reading a newspaper.

 **Unit 3** **I Want A Red Skirt**

check box	
parents	
teacher	

New Vocabularies

blouse	blouse	pants	pants
cap	cap	red	red
necktie	necktie	blue	blue
skirt	skirt	white	white
sandals	sandals	black	black
jeans	jeans	pink	pink
shorts	shorts	yellow	yellow
sneakers	sneakers		
yellow green	yellow green		

gray	gray	was	was
navy	navy	the	the
brown	brown	to	to
it	it	little	little
to	to	have	have

New Expressions

I want a red skirt.

What color do you want?

I will try red.

Unit 4 **I Get Up At 7:40 In The Morning**

	check box
parents	
teacher	

New Vocabularies

what	what	night	night
time	time	wash	wash
get up	get up	breakfast	breakfast
morning	morning	lunch	lunch
afternoon	afternoon	dinner	dinner

Express Yourself

do my homework   do my homework

go to school   go to school   am   am

go to bed   go to bed   run   run

brush   brush   fast   fast

late   late   down   down

I   I   has   has

What time do you get up?

I get up at 8 o'clock.

I do my homework in the afternoon.

Unit 5 I Go To Church Every Sunday

	check box
parents	
teacher	

New Vocabularies

Monday   Monday   Tuesday   Tuesday

Wednesday   Wednesday

Thursday Thursday

Friday Friday   me   me

Saturday Saturday   up   up

Sunday Sunday   on   on

play the piano play the piano

paint paint   off   off

water the plants water the plants

take a ballet lesson take a ballet lesson

go to the library go to the library

read books read books

go hiking go hiking

my my   jump jump

New Expressions

What do you do on Sundays?

I go to church on Sundays.

I have a science class on Wednesdays.

Unit 6 I Like Sunny Days

New Vocabularies

windy	windy	fly a kite	fly a kite
sunny	sunny	thunder	thunder
foggy	foggy	went	went
stormy	stormy	had	had
cloudy	cloudy	good	good
rainy	rainy	stop	stop
snowy	snowy	get	get
walk outside	walk outside	got	got
play board games	play board games		
make a snowman	make a snowman		

New Expressions

What kind of weather do you like?

I like sunny days.

I can swim in the warm sunlight.

 **Unit 7**

The Months June, July And August Are In The Summer

	check box
parents	
teacher	

New Vocabularies

January	January	winter	winter		
February	February	summer	summer		
March	March	warm	warm		
April	April	hot	hot		
May	May	cool	cool		
June	June	windy	windy		
July	July	snowy	snowy		
August	August	cold	cold		
September	September	like	like		
October	October	don't	don't		
November	November	and	and		
December	December	father	father		
spring	spring	friend	friend		
fall	fall	do	do	did	did

New Expressions

I can swim at the beach in the summer.

I can go on a picnic in spring.

It's cool and windy in fall.

Unit 8 Lizards Live In The Desert

check box	
parents	
teacher	

New Vocabularies

frog	frog	cave	cave
bat	bat	ocean	ocean
whale	whale	in	in
sheep	sheep	out	out
camel	camel	ran	ran
pigeon	pigeon	play	play
city	city	one	one
grassy fields	grassy fields		
pond	pond	two	two

New Expressions

Where do camels live?

They live in the desert.

I want to have a lizard.

Unit 9 I Live In Italy

	check box
parents	
teacher	

New Vocabularies

America	America	China	China
American	American	Asia	Asia
Europe	Europe	Chinese	Chinese
English	English	Japan	Japan
the UK	the UK	Asia	Asia
Canada	Canada	Japanese	Japanese
Canadian	Canadian	France	France
Australia	Australia	French	French
Australian	Australian	Ethiopia	Ethiopia
Oceania	Oceania	Africa	Africa

xpress ourself

Ethiopian	Ethiopian		
yes	yes	we	we
no	no	they	they
you	you	are	are

New Expressions

Where do you live?

I live in Italy.

Italy is in Europe.

Unit 10 — I Have A Sandwich And Orange Juice For Lunch

	check box
parents	
teacher	

New Vocabularies

breakfast	breakfast	bacon	bacon
lunch	lunch	milk	milk
dinner	dinner	sandwich	sandwich
scrambled eggs	scrambled eggs		

juice	juice	salad	salad
chicken	chicken	pie	pie
fruit	fruit	not	not
hamburger	hamburger	ate	ate
cereal	cereal	be	be
spaghetti	spaghetti	day	day
soup	soup	three	three
steak	steak	four	four

New Expressions

What are you having for dinner?

I have a sandwich and juice.

What do you eat for breakfast?

Unit 11 It Tastes Sweet

	check box
parents	
teacher	

New Vocabularies

French fries	French fries
medicine	medicine

lemon	lemon	of	of
greasy	greasy		
bitter	bitter	sit	sit
sour	sour	sat	sat
red pepper	red pepper		
cookies	cookies	look	look
sausage	sausage		
hot	hot		
sweet	sweet		
salty	salty	night	night
taste	taste	rain	rain

New Expressions

What does it taste like?

How does it taste?

It tastes bitter.

Unit 12 I Want To Swim At The Swimming Pool

	check box
parents	
teacher	

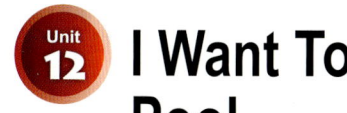

New Vocabularies

bookstore — bookstore

toy store — toy store

swimming pool — swimming pool

department store — department store

flower shop — flower shop

eat — eat

theater — theater

for — for

beauty salon — beauty salon

if — if

post office — post office

from — from

grocery store — grocery store

pharmacy — pharmacy

five — five

library — library

six — six

New Expressions

Where can I buy a book?

You can buy one at the bookstore.

Let's go to the department store.

I Want To Ride The Merry-Go-Round

	check box
parents	
teacher	

Unit 13

New Vocabularies

merry-go-round — merry-go-round

amusement park — amusement park

roller coaster — roller coaster   book — book

miniature railway — miniature railway

log flume — log flume   go — go

spinning cups — spinning cups

bumper cards — bumper cards

ferries wheel — ferries wheel

motion simulator — motion simulator

pirate ship — pirate ship

can — can   new — new

car — car   green — green

New Expressions

What do you want to ride?

I want to ride the merry-go-round.

I'm so excited.

	check box
Unit 14 **I Like To Play With Toys But I Don't Like To Clean Up**	
parents	
teacher	

New Vocabularies

play with toys	play with toys		
take a science class	take a science class		
water the plants	water the plants		
study at school	study at school		
do homework at home	do homework at home		
play the piano	play the piano		
take a bath	take a bath		
play computer games	play computer games		
go hiking	go hiking	seen	seen
clean up	clean up	that	that
red	red	saw	saw
see	see	eight	eight

New Expressions

I like to read English story books.

I don't like to dance in ballet class.

I like to take care of my baby sister.

Unit 15 My Leg Is Longer Than Your Leg

	check box
parents	
teacher	

New Vocabularies

bigger	bigger	faster	faster
heavier	heavier	slower	slower
healthier	healthier	want	want
higher	higher	this	this
smaller	smaller	yellow	yellow
taller	taller	give	give
longer	longer	come	come
shorter	shorter	came	came
more beautiful	more beautiful		

New Expressions

The elephant is bigger than the rabbit.

I am taller than my brother.

My father is heavier than my baby sister.

	check box
parents	
teacher	

Unit 16 **The Lion Is The Strongest Among Us**

New Vocabularies

biggest	biggest
smallest	smallest
shortest	shortest
slowest	slowest
fastest	fastest
strongest	strongest
tallest	tallest

will	will	blue	blue
old	old	nine	nine
with	with	ten	ten

Are you the tallest here?

Yes, I am.

I am the youngest in my family.

Test 1
Unit 1-Unit 8

SCORE OF THE TEST		
LISTENING	/	7
READING	/	8
WRITING	/	5
TOTAL	/	20

Listening Test L

 82

1. 다음 대화를 잘 듣고 주어진 질문에 알맞은 답을 고르세요.

❶ 　❷ 　❸

2. 다음 대화를 잘 듣고 주어진 질문에 알맞은 답을 고르세요.

❶  7:40　❷  8:00　❸ 8:20

3. 다음 대화를 잘 듣고 주어진 질문에 알맞은 답을 고르세요.

❶ 　❷ 　❸

4. 다음 대화를 잘 듣고 주어진 질문에 알맞은 답을 고르세요.

❶ 　❷

83

5. 대화를 듣고 엄마가 어디에
   있는지 찾으세요.

6. 대화를 잘 듣고 ✔ 또는 ✕에
   동그라미 하세요.

7. 잘 듣고 들은 순서대로 알파벳을
   쓰세요.

Reading Test R

8. 빈칸에 들어갈 단어로 바르게
   짝지어진 것을 고르세요.

This is my brother's backpack. He has ___ book, ___ notebook, ____ orange colored pencil, and ____ eraser.

❶ a – a – a – an
❷ an – an – a – a
❸ an – a – a – an
❹ a – a – an – an

9. 질문에 알맞은 답을 고르세요.

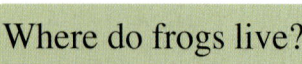 Where do frogs live?

❶ I live on the third floor.
❷ She is in the kitchen. She is cooking.
❸ They live in a pond.

10. 다음을 읽고 알맞은 그림을 고르세요.

11. 그림에 맞는 표현을 고르세요.

12. 문장의 빈칸에 알맞은 단어를 연결하세요.

13. 다음의 부분 대화들을 읽고 순서에 맞게 번호를 쓰세요.

14. 다음 그림을 보고 그림과 일치하지 않는 답을 고르세요.

Alice: Who is your brother?
Jeff: My brother is tall and strong.

① ② ③

Spring is (cool / warm).
I like to (go on a picnic / swim in the pool) in spring.

Winter is (cold / cool).
I like to (fly a kite / make a snowman) in winter.

Yesterday was Sunday.
I _____ to the zoo.

• go

Today is Monday.
I _____ to school.

• went

I'm looking for a necktie.

I want blue.

What color do you want?

What are you looking for?

1. Megan's grandma is cooking in the kitchen.
2. Megan's grandpa is watching TV in the living room.
3. Megan's sister eating lunch in the dining room.

Whales live in the ocean.

15. 문장을 읽고 그림을 그리세요.

Writing Test ®

16. 그림을 보고 빈칸에 알맞은 단어를 쓰세요.

17. 그림을 보고 알맞은 단어를 쓰세요.

WORD BOX red jeans   green shorts   sky blue sneakers

 I want _____.

 My grandpa and grandma are eating lunch in the _____ _____.

 My brother is taking a bath in the _____.

18. 문장을 완성하세요.

1. wise / My / kind / is / uncle / . / and

➡ _____

2. you / go / school / What / ? / do / time / to

➡ _____

19. 빈칸을 채워서 질문에 답하세요.

Question: What months are in the summer?
Answe: The months _____,
_____, and _____ are
in the summer.

WORD BOX

September   March
June   November
August   May
July   February

20. 그림을 보고 빈칸에 알맞은 단어를 쓰세요.

WORD BOX

goes   down
up   out

Jeff goes _____.   Max _____ into the classroom.
Megan goes _____.   Alice comes _____ of the classroom.

Name :

SCORE OF THE TEST		
LISTENING	/	6
READING	/	9
WRITING	/	5
TOTAL	/	20

Test 2
Unit 9-Unit 16

Listening Test L

1. 잘 듣고 일치하는 그림에
   동그라미 하세요.

❶ ❷

2. 대화를 듣고 알맞은 답을
   고르세요.

❶  Alice ❷  Max ❸  Megan

3. 잘 듣고 들은 순서대로
   알파벳을 쓰세요.

4. 잘 듣고 맞는 것끼리
   연결하세요.

ⓐ •

ⓑ •

5. 잘 듣고 소리 나는 곳에 들어갈
   알맞은 단어를 찾아 동그라미
   하세요.

❶ with   ❷ from   ❸ can   ❹ by

6. 대화를 듣고 알맞은
   나라 국기를 고르세요.

 ❶    ❷    ❸

Reading Test   Ⓡ

7. 그림에 맞는 표현을 고르세요.

I like to ride the
(merry-go-round / ferries wheel).

I want to ride the
(roller coaster / spinning cups).

8. 주어진 질문에 알맞은 답을
   고르세요.

Where can I buy a book?

❶ At the bookstore. It's near the corner.
❷ The book is Megan's.
❸ I want to buy fruits, too. Let's go together.

9. 읽고 알맞은 그림을 고르세요.

Lisa: Which ruler is yours?
Max: My ruler is longer than yours, but it is shorter than Scott's.

A   B   C

10. 주어진 문장으로 대화가
    시작하도록 순서에 맞게
    번호를 쓰세요.

Who is the tallest animal in this picture?

No, the giraffe is the tallest one.

The tiger is the tallest in this picture.

11. 빈칸에 알맞은 단어로
    짝지어진 것을 고르세요.

I will go to the swimming pool _____ my family. _____ will go there by _____.

❶ for – We – bus   ❷ for – They
❸ with – We – car   ❹ with– They – red

12. 빈칸에 들어갈 알맞은 단어를
연결하세요.

Is she your sister?
She _____s pretty.   •   • see

After wearing glasses,
I can _____ well.   •   • look

13. 그림에 맞는 문장이 되도록
알맞은 단어를 고르세요.

 The chocolate tastes (salty / sweet).

 The red pepper tastes (hot / sour).

14. 다음 그림을 보고 그림과
일치하는 문장의 번호를 써
넣으세요.

A     B

1. I like to play soccer, but I don't like to do my homework.
2. I like to ride a pirate ship, but I don't like to ride spinning cups.

15. 대화 순서에 맞게 번호를
쓰세요.

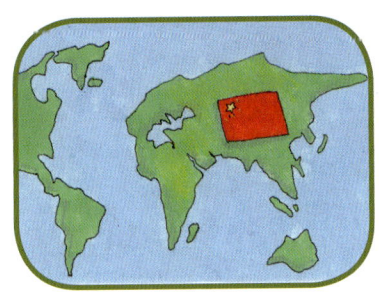

I live in China.

China is in Asia.

Where do you live?

Where is China?

Writing Test ⓡ

16. 문장을 완성해 보세요.

1. at the flower shop / buy / Scott / . / some flowers / wants to

➡ _____

2. a / I / to / . / bumper car / ride / want

➡ _____

17. 그림을 보고 알맞은 단어를 쓰세요.

Bob's mom is _____ than my mom.
My mom is _____ than Bob's mom.

Alice's backpack is _____ than Max's.
Max's backpack is _____ than Alice's.

18. 그림을 보고 빈칸에 알맞은 단어를 쓰세요.

WORD BOX

milk salad
cookies cereal
juice hamburger

What do you eat for breakfast?
I eat _____, _____, and _____ for breakfast.

What do you eat for lunch?
I eat a _____, _____, and _____ for lunch.

19. 그림을 보고 빈칸에 알맞은 단어를 쓰세요

I live in _____.
_____ is in _____.

WORD BOX the USA Australia Canada England Asia Europe

20. 빈칸을 채워서 질문에 답하세요.

What do you like to do?

I like to _____,
but I don't like to _____.

Final Test
Unit 1-Unit 16

Listening Test L

SCORE OF THE TEST		
LISTENING	/	7
READING	/	8
WRITING	/	5
TOTAL	/	20

86

1. 대화를 듣고 올바른 답을 고르세요.

❶
department store/
On Orange Street

❷
toy store/
On Apple Street

❸
department store/
On Apple Street

2. 잘 듣고 키가 가장 큰 사람을 고르세요.

❶    ❷    ❸

3. 대화를 듣고 그림과 일치히면 T, 일치하지 않으면 F에 동그라미 하세요.

A  T / F

B  T / F

4. 대화를 잘 듣고 알맞은 답을 고르세요.

❶    ❷    ❸

5. 잘 듣고 내용에 맞게 시각을 표시하세요.

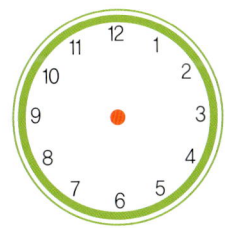

Final Test

6. 대화를 잘 듣고 질문에 알맞은 그림을 고르세요.

❶   ❷   ❸

7. 대화를 잘 듣고 질문에 알맞은 그림을 고르세요.

❶ January 1   ❷ December 12   ❸ October 10   ❹ August 8

Reading Test Ⓡ

8. 빈칸에 들어갈 단어를 골라 알맞게 연결하세요.

Watch _____! There is a rock. •   • ⓐ for

Can you sing a song _____ me? •   • ⓑ will

It _____ be sunny tomorrow. •   • ⓒ out

9. 빈칸에 들어갈 알맞은 단어로 짝지어진 것을 고르세요.

I have a red pepper sandwich, cookies and lemon juice for lunch. The sandwich is _____, cookies are sweet and lemon juice is _____.

❶ bitter – salty   ❷ hot – bitter   ❸ hot – sour

10. 주어진 문장으로 대화가 시작하도록 순서에 맞게 번호를 쓰세요.

Where is mom?

She is bathing the baby.

What is she doing in the bathroom?

Mom is in the bathroom.

Final Test

11. 다음 대화를 읽고 알맞은 그림을 고르세요.

Max: Where does this animal live?
Tina: It lives in the desert.
Max: Is it smaller than a horse?
Tina: No, it is bigger than a horse.

12. 다음 그림을 보고 그림과 일치하는 문장의 번호를 써 넣으세요.

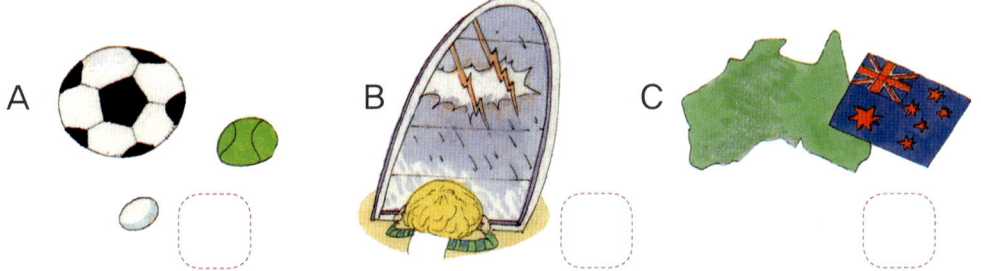

A   B   C

1. It's lightning outside. It's scary.
2. I live in Australia. It's in Oceania.
3. The soccer ball is the biggest among three.

13. 그림에 맞는 표현을 동그라미 하세요.

I want (shorts / jeans / a skirt),
and (a yellow hat / a navy hair band /
an orange cap).

I don't like to cat (cookics / fruit salad).

14. 다음 빈칸에 공통으로 들어갈 알맞은 단어를 고르세요.

In spring we can go ＿＿ a picnic.
At night I turn ＿＿ the light.

❶ of   ❷ on   ❸ by

15. 다음의 글을 읽고 내용에 알맞은 그림자 그림을 고르세요.

I wanted to ride the merry-go-round.
But my brother didn't like it.
So we lined up to ride the roller coaster together.

A   B

16. 그림을 보고 내용에 알맞게 빈칸을 채워 보세요.

My mom checked the weather forecast and she gave me a yellow umbrella and a green rain coat.

It's _____ today.

WORD BOX snowy / windy / sunny / rainy / cloudy

Max   Jeff   Bob

Bob is the _____ among three.

17. 그림을 보고 빈칸을 채워 문장을 완성하세요.

1. the / Whales / . / ocean / live / in

➡ _____

2. want to / I / mail / . / in the post office / a / letter

➡ _____

18. 문장을 바르게 완성해 보세요.

19. 그림을 보고 알맞은 단어를 쓰세요.

I live in _____.   I live in _____.
It is in _____.   It is in _____.

WORD BOX

the UK	English
Canada	Canadian
France	French
America	American
Asia	Europe

20. 표를 보고 빈칸에 알맞은 단어를 쓰세요.

7:35	7:40	8:00	8:20	9:00
get up	brush one's teeth	eat breakfast	go to school	study English

At seven forty,

I _____.

 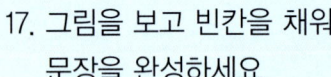

Unit 1

Page 6
Let's Practice!
1) B
I have a brother. He is short and fat.
2) B
I have a sister Amy. She looks pretty and short.
3) A
I have an uncle. He studies very hard. He looks so smart.

Page 7
Check & Check
1) a / He / a
2) an / She / an
3) a / an / an
4) a / an / a

Page 9
Let's Do It At Home
1.
1) B
My mom is short and very strong.
2) A
My brother is tall and lazy. He usually sits on a chair.

2.
1) My grandfather looks old and thin.
2) My sister looks tall and pretty.
3) My father looks fat and tall.

3.
an / aunt / She / a / She / She / an

Unit 2

Page 12
Let's Practice!
ANSWERS) 4 − 3 − 2 − 1
1) My brother is cleaning up his bedroom.
2) My uncle is fixing the car outside.
3) My grandma is watching TV in the living room.
4) My mom is feeding the baby in the dining room.

Page 13
Check & Check
ANSWERS)
1. goes / by
2. goes / by
3. is / at
4. has / at
5. has / as / as
6. is / as / as

ANSWERS)
is / at / by / has / goes / as

Page 15
Let's Do It At Home
1.
1) goes
2) as
3) by
4) is
5) has
6) at

2.
1) c
2) a
3) b

Answers

3.
1) What is your mom doing?
2) She is cleaning in the bedroom.

Unit 3

Page 18
Let's Practice!
1) B
Woman: What are you looking for?
Boy: I'm looking for a blue necktie.
2) B
Man: May I help you?
Girl: I want yellow pants.
3) B
Woman: May I help you?
Girl: I want a pink dotted skirt.

Page 19
Check & Check
1. was / at
2. was / have
3. is / the / a
4. have / is / little

ANSWERS)
have / to / was / little / the / it

Page 21
Let's Do It At Home
1. Alice / Tina / Bob / Scott
2.
1) was / is
2) have / has
3.

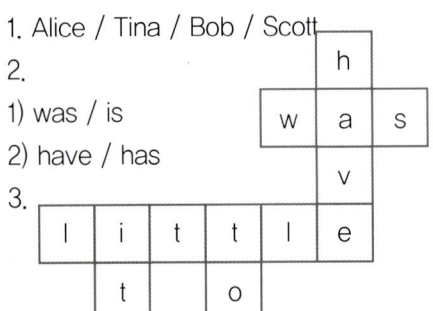

Unit 4

Page 24
Let's Practice!
1) X
Boy: What time do you wash your face?
Girl: I wash my face at 7:50.
2) O
Boy: What time do you eat lunch?
Girl: I eat lunch at 12:30.
3) X
Girl: What time do you play soccer?
Boy: I play soccer at 4:40.
4) X
Girl: What time do you go to bed?
Boy: I go to bed at 10:20.

Page 25
Check & Check
1) have / has
2) am / run
3) down / up

ANSWERS)
am / run / fast / down / has / have

Page 27
Let's Do It At Home
1) b
I brush my teeth at 8:20.
2) d
I have lunch at 12:10.
3) c
I go to bed at 9:50.
4) a
I have dinner at 7:50.

ANSWERS)

1. X 2. V 3. V

ANSWERS)
1. go to school
2. watch TV
3. study English

Unit 5

Page 30
Let's Practice!
1) B
Girl: What do you do on Thursdays?
Boy: I play baseball every Thursday.
2) A
Boy: What does your brother do on Saturdays?
Girl: He goes to art class every Saturday.
3) B
Girl: What does your grandma do every Sunday?
Boy: She cooks for my family every Sunday.

Page 31
Check & Check
1) jump / on
2) out / my
3) out / on
4) me

ANSWERS)
up / my / on / me / jump / off

Page 33
Let's Do It At Home
1.
1) B
Girl: What does he do on Sundays?
Boy: He goes to church every Sunday.
2) B
Boy: What do you do on Mondays?

Girl: I play the piano every Monday.
2.
1) My grandma cooks for me every Sunday.
2) I take a ballet lesson on Thursdays.
3) What does he do on Saturdays?
3.
me / my / on / my / off / my / My / jump / My / up

Unit 6

Page 36
Let's Practice!
1. 1–4–2–3
1) I like rainy days because I like to wear my yellow rain boots.
2) I like stormy days because I can play board games with my family.
3) I can fly a kite on windy days.
4) I don't like foggy days because I cannot see the city well.

Page 37
Check & Check
1. went / stop
2. got
3. good / get

ANSWERS)

Answers

Page 39
Let's Do It At Home
1.
1) had
2) got
3) went
4) get
5) stop
6) good

2.
1) b
2) a
3) c

3.
1) What kind of weather do you like?
2) I can swim on sunny days.

Unit 7

Page 42
Let's Practice!
1) A
Boy: Winter is cold. I can make a snowman in the winter.
2) B
Girl: I can see colorful flowers in the spring. It's warm in spring.
3) B
Girl: The months December, January, and February are in the winter.

Page 43
Check & Check
1. father's / and / mother's
2. Do / don't / father
3. did / friend's

4. do / and

Page 45
Let's Do It At Home
1. 4 – 1 – 3 – 2
2.
1) Do / don't / Do / do
2) did / father / friend
3.

			f	r	i	e	n	d
	d		a					i
d	o	n	'	t		a	n	d
			h					
			e					
			r					

Unit 8

Page 48
Let's Practice!
1) X
Girl: What lives in a pond?
Boy: Frogs live in a pond.
2) X
Boy: Where do camels live?
Girl: They live in the desert.
3) O
Girl: Where do bats live?
Boy: They live in a cave.
4) O
Boy: Who lives in the ocean?
Girl: Whales live in the ocean.

Page 49
Check & Check
1) ran / out / in
2) ran / play
3) one / two

4) In / two / one / one
5) one / ran

ANSWERS)
one–in–out–two–ran–play

Page 50

1) ocean
2) forest
3) cave
4) desert
5) grassy fields
6) snow
7) pond
8) city

Page 51

Let's Do It At Home

1.

1) a
Boy: What lives in the desert?
Girl: Camels live in the desert.
2) d
Boy: Where do skunks live?
Girl: They live in the forest.
3) b
Boy: What lives in the snow?
Girl: Polar bears live in the snow.
4) c
Boy: Where do sheep live?
Girl: They live in grassy fields.

2.
1) X
2) X
3) V

3.
1) Whales live
2) Frogs live

3) Lizards live

Unit 9

Page 54

Let's Practice!

1) B
Boy: Hi, I live in China. China is in Asia. This is the Chinese flag.
2) A
Girl: Hello, I live in Australia. I'm Australian. It's in Oceania. This is the Australian flag.
3) B
Boy: Hi, I'm Korean. But I live in Canada. This is the Canadian flag.

Page 55

Check & Check

1) We / are
2) are
3) we
4) No / you

ANSWERS)
they / are / we / you / no / yes

Page 57

Let's Do It At Home

1.

1) A
I live in France. France is in Europe. In France you can see the Tower Eiffel.
2) A
I'm Australian. Australia is in Oceania. I sometimes visit the Opera house.

2.
1) c
This is the Italian flag.

Answers

2) a
This is the American flag.
3) b
I live in China. China is in Asia.
3.
you / Yes / We / are / we

Unit 10

Page 60
Let's Practice!
3–2–4–1
1)
Boy: What do you eat for breakfast?
Girl: I eat scrambled eggs and bacon.
2)
Woman: What do you eat for dinner?
Boy: I eat chicken and salad for dinner.
3)
Woman: What do eat for breakfast?
Girl: I eat a bowl of cereal, milk and fruit.
4)
Man: What do you eat for lunch?
Girl: I eat a sandwich and orange juice.

Page 61
Check & Check
1) ate
2) Be / not
3) ate / three / four / be
4) day
5) not

ANSWERS)
ate / not / be / three / four / day

Page 63

Let's Do It At Home
1.
1) ate
2) three
3) day
4) not
5) four
6) be

2.
1) b
2) c
3) a

3.
1) What do you eat for breakfast?
2) I eat salad and steak for dinner.

Unit 11

Page 66
Let's Practice!
1.
1) sweet / sour
Woman: Do you like lemonade?
Boy: Yes, I do.
Woman: How does it taste?
Boy: It tastes sweet but sour.

2) sweet / bitter
Man: What would you like to have?
Girl: I want to have a cup of coffee. I like something bitter and sweet.

3) hot
Woman: Do you like bacon?
Girl: No, I don't. I like salsa with chili sauce.

Woman: What does it taste like?

Girl: It tastes like red peppers.

Page 67

Check & Check

1.

1) look

2) sat / night / rain

3) sit / look

4) night / of / of

ANSWERS)

of / rain / night / sit / look / sat

Page 69

Let's Do It At Home

1. 4–1–2–3

2.

1) Sit / Look

2) night / of / rain

3.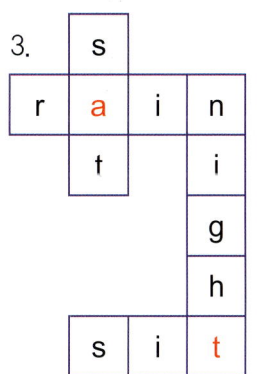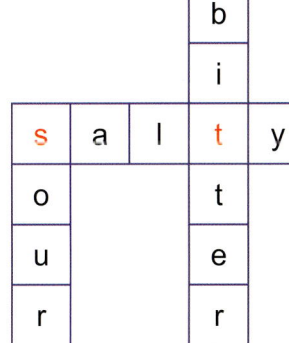

Unit 12

Page 72

Let's Practice!

1) O

Girl: I want to buy some vegetables at the grocery store.

2) X

Boy: I want to watch a movie with my girl friend.

3) O

Girl: Before I join my friend's birthday party, I want to have my hair cut.

4) X

Boy: I want to read some story books at the library this afternoon.

Page 73

Check & Check

1) If / eat

2) from / for

3) five / for

ANSWERS)

if / five / eat / from / for / six

Page 75

Let's Do It At Home

1.

1) d

I want to buy some flowers. Where can I buy them?

2) a

I want to buy a book. Where can I buy one?

3) b

I want to mail a letter. Where can I mail a letter?

4) c

I want to go swimming. Where can I go swimming?

2.

1) X

2) X

3) V

3.

1) buy some vegetables

2) mail a letter

3) see a movie

Answers

Unit 13

Page 78
Let's Practice!
1) A
Boy: What do you want to do?
Girl: I want to ride the ferries wheel.
2) A
Girl: What do you want to ride?
Boy: I want to ride a pirate ship.
3) B
Boy: What do you want to ride?
Girl: I want to ride a log flume.

Page 79
Check & Check
1) can / go
2) green / book
3) book
4) car

ANSWERS)
go / green / can / book / car / new

Page 81
Let's Do It At Home
1.
1) A
Girl: I want to ride a motion simulator.
Boy: That's so exciting!
2) B
Girl: I want to see the view from high up.
Boy: You can ride the ferries wheel.

2.
1) I want to ride a roller coaster.
2) I want to go home and sleep.
3) I want to ride a pirate ship.

ANSWERS)
go / new / green / go

Unit 14

Page 84
Let's Practice!
3–2–4–1
1) boy: I like to play soccer with my friends.
2) girl: I don't like to paint.
3) boy: I like to play computer games.
4) girl: I like to go hiking.

Page 85
Check & Check
1. see / that
2. red
3. eight / seven
4. saw / seven
5. eight

ANSWERS)
seven–see–that–saw–eight–red

Page 87
Let's Do It At Home
1.
1) see
2) red
3) eight
4) that
5) saw
6) seven

2.
1) c
2) a
3) b

3.

1) I don't like to water the plants.

2) Don't you clean up your room?

Unit 15

Page 90

Let's Practice!

1) A

Woman: Which is longer?

Boy: My pencil is longer than Alice's pencil.

2) B

Girl: Scott, which is healthier?

Boy: Pam's plant is healthier than my plant.

3) A

Boy: Which is fatter?

Girl: The boy is fatter than the girl.

Page 91

Check & Check

1) want / come

2) yellow

3) came / come

ANSWERS)

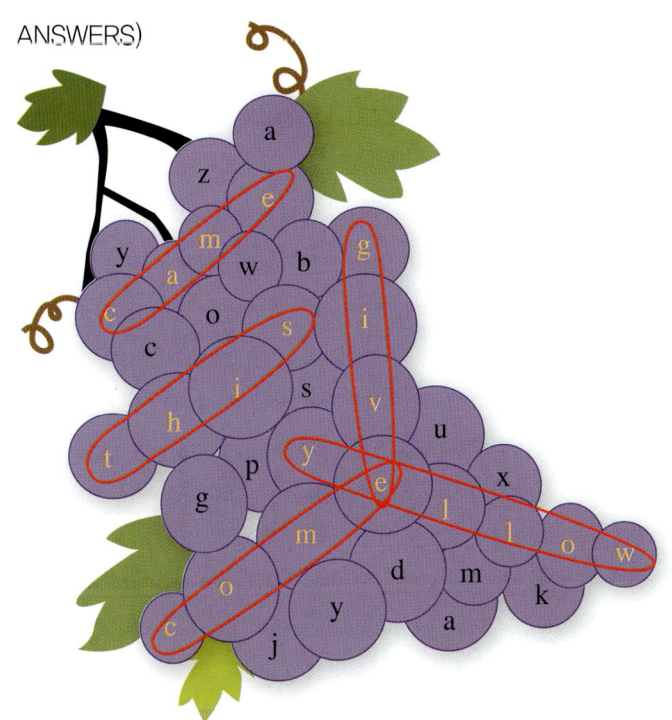

Page 93

Let's Do It At Home

1.

1) O

2) X

3) O

4) O

2.

1) came / come

2) want / yellow / give

3.

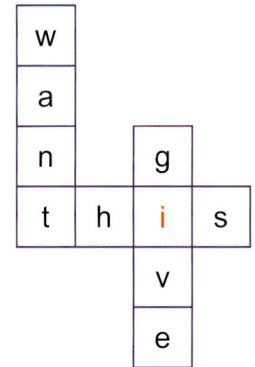

		w			
		a			
		n		g	
	t	h	i	s	
				v	
				e	

		c	a	m	e
y	e	l	l	o	w
				m	
				e	

Unit 16

Page 96

Let's Practice!

1) O

Girl: Which backpack is the biggest among the three?

Boy: Pam's backpack is the biggest.

2) X

Boy: Which pencil is the shortest among the four?

Girl: The yellow pencil is the shortest.

3) X

Answers

Girl: Who is the oldest in Tina's family?

Boy: Tina's father is the oldest.

4) O

Boy: Who is the slowest among the three?

Girl: The skunk is the slowest.

Page 97
Check & Check

1) nine

2) blue

3) will / with

4) ten

ANSWERS)

old / blue / with / will / ten / nine

Page 98

1. longest

2. shortest

3. fastest

4. slowest

5. tallest

6. smallest

Page 99
Let's Do It At Home

1.

1) d

Mom bought me a back pack six years ago. Now it has become (old: beep sound).

2) c

Boy: Which do you like, the mountain or the sea?

Girl: I like the sea. Because I like the color (blue: beep sound).

3) a

There were ten monkeys in the room. One went back to his home. Now there are (nine: beep sound) monkeys.

4) b

Girl: Do you go to school alone?

Boy: No. I go to school (with: beep sound) my friends.

2.

1) X

2) X

3) V

3.

1) Scott is the strongest.

2) Bob is the tallest.

3) Tina is the shortest.

Test 1(Unit 1 – Unit 8)

Page 119
Listening Test

1) 3

Boy: What do you do on Mondays?

Girl: I take a painting lesson on Mondays. What about you?

Boy: I have a baseball match on Mondays.

＊Question: What does boy do on Mondays?

2) 2

Girl: What time do you get up?

Boy: I get up at 7:40 in the morning.

Girl: What time do you eat breakfast?

Boy: I eat breakfast at 8 o'clock.

＊Question: What time does he eat breakfast?

3) 2

Girl: This is my sister. Her name is Grace. She is tall and pretty. She is very smart, too.

＊Question: Who is Grace?

4) 2

Man: Where do Polar bears live?
Girl: They live in the snow.
Man: Where do Lizards live?
Girl: They live in the desert.
＊Question: Who lives in the desert?

5) 2
Boy: Is mom in the kitchen?
Girl: No, she isn't.
Boy: Where is dad?
Girl: He's in the garden.
Boy: What is he doing?
Girl: He's watering the plants.
　Oh, mom is in the garden, too.

6)
1) X
Man: What are you looking for?
Girl: I want a hat.
Man: What color do you want?
Girl: I will try blue.

2) V
Woman: What are you looking for?
Boy: I want a T-shirt.
Woman: What color do you want?
Boy: I will try orange.

7) b-a
a) The months December, January and February are in this season.
b) The months June, July and August are in this season.

Reading Test
8) 4
9) 3
10) 1
11)
warm / go on a picnic
cold / make a snowman

12) went / go
13) 2-4-3-1
14) 3
15) 고래를 두 마리 이상 그림.

Writing test
16) sky blue sneakers

17) dining room / bathroom

18)
1. My uncle is wise and kind.
2. What time do you go to school?

19) June / July / August

20)
Jeff goes down.
Megan goes up.
Max goes into the classroom.
Alice comes out of the classroom.

Test 2 (Unit 9 - Unit 16)

Page 123
Listening Test
1) 2
Boy: I like to play soccer, and I don't like to clean up my room.

2) 3
Girl: What are they doing?
Boy: They are running.
Girl: Who is the fastest among them?
Boy: I don't know. Maybe Max.
Girl: No, look at that! Megan comes the first. She is the fastest!

3) b-a

Answers

a. Bob is stronger than Max.

b. The yellow pencil is longer than the green pencil.

4) a–dinner / b–lunch

a)

Man: What do you eat for lunch?

Girl: I eat a sandwich, an apple, and orange juice for lunch.

b)

Woman: What do you eat for dinner?

Boy: I eat chicken, salad, soup and rice for dinner.

5) 2

Boy: Where are you (beep)?

Girl: I'm (beep) the U.S.A.

6) 3

Boy: Alice, where are you from?

Girl: I'm from Italy. This is the Italian flag. Dan, where are you from?

Boy: I'm from the U.S.A.

＊Question: Where is Alice from?

Reading Test

7) ferries wheel / roller coaster

8) 1

9) B

10) 2–1

11) 3

12) look / see

13) sweet / hot

14) 2 – 1

15) 2–4–1–3

Writing Test

16)

1. Scott wants to buy some flowers at the flower shop.

2. I want to ride a bumper car.

17)

taller /shorter

bigger / smaller

18)

salad, milk, cereal / hamburger, juice, cookies

19) England / England / Europe

20) dance / sing

Final Test

Page 127

Listening Test

1) 3

Girl: I'm going to buy a cute doll for my sister. Her birthday is coming.

Boy: Where will you buy one?

Girl: Department store. There is a big toy section. Do you want to go with me?

Boy: Sure.

Girl: But I'm not sure where it is.

Boy: I know. It's on Apple Street.

＊Question: Where will they go?

2) 1

Girl: I'm Alice. My brother Ben is smaller than me. My sister Kate is taller than me.

Who is the tallest?

3) T / F

A. Boy: Where is dad?

Woman: He is in the living room.

Boy: Is he reading a newspaper?

Woman: No, he's watching T.V.

B. Man: May I help you? What do you want?

Girl: I want to buy a skirt.

Man: What color do you want?

Girl: I want to try blue.

4) 2

Boy: What kind of weather do you like?

Girl: I like sunny because I can swim at the beach.

Boy: I like snowy.

Girl: Why?

Boy: Because I can make a snowman.

＊Question: What kind of weather does the boy like?

5) 12:30

I have lunch at 12:30 in the afternoon

6) 3

Boy: Let's go outside.

Girl: What are we going to do?

Boy: We are going to fly a kite and play soccer.

Girl: I like to fly a kite, but I don't like to play soccer.

＊Question: What does the girl like to do?

7) August

Boy: It's very hot outside.

Girl: Yes, it's the middle of summer.

Boy: I don't like summer. It's too hot.

Girl: But we can go to swim at the beach. That's why I like summer.

＊Question: When is it now? Choose what month it is.

Reading Test

8) c–a–b

9) 3

10) 3 – 2 – 1

11) 2

12) 3 – 1 – 2

13)

jeans / an orange cap

fruit salad

14) 2

15) B

16) rainy

17) strongest

18)

1) Whales live in the ocean.

2) I want to mail a letter in the post office.

19)

Canada – America – Italy – Europe

20)

brush my teeth

Get Ready Jump 1

2nd Printing 2014.11.20

Author : Samuel Lee / Hyunjee Shim

Supervisor : LLS English Research Center

Publisher : Kiseon Lee

Publishing Company: JPLUS

467-30 Mangwon-dong, Mapo-gu, Seoul, Korea

Telephone : 02-332-8320

Fax : 02-332-8321

Homepage : www.jplus114.com

Registration Number : 10-1680

Registration Date : 1998.12.09

ISBN 978-89-94632-11-7(63740)

© JPLUS 2010